Cambridge Latin Course

Book II
Teacher's Guide

FOURTH EDITION

CAMBRIDGE
UNIVERSITY PRESS

PUBLISHED BY THE PRESS SYNDICATE OF THE UNIVERSITY OF CAMBRIDGE
The Pitt Building, Trumpington Street, Cambridge, United Kingdom

CAMBRIDGE UNIVERSITY PRESS
The Edinburgh Building, Cambridge CB2 2RU, UK
40 West 20th Street, New York, NY 10011–4211, USA
10 Stamford Road, Oakleigh, VIC 3166, Australia
Ruiz de Alarcón 13, 28014 Madrid, Spain
Dock House, The Waterfront, Cape Town 8001, South Africa

http://www.cambridge.org

This book, an outcome of work jointly commissioned by the Schools Council
before its closure and the Cambridge School Classics Project, is published under
the aegis of Qualifications and Curriculum Authority Enterprises Limited,
29 Bolton Street, London W1Y 7PD.

First published 1971
Second edition 1983
This edition 2000

Printed in the United Kingdom at the University Press, Cambridge

Typeface *10.75/13.5pt Palatino*   System *QuarkXPress®*

A catalogue record for this book is available from the British Library

ISBN 0 521 64467 4 paperback

Layout by Newton Harris Design Partnership
Illustration by Kathy Baxendale

ACKNOWLEDGEMENTS

For help in preparing Book II of the *Cambridge Latin Course* and this
Teacher's Guide we should like to express our thanks to the following: Jill
Dalladay for her work on the Guide; members of the Project's Working
Party: Eileen Emmett, Jean Hubbard and Pam Perkins; Maire Collins for
typing and formatting the text; and for assistance of various kinds: Patricia
Acres, Roger Davies, William Duggan, Lynda Goss, Robin Griffin, Debbie
James, Brian Milligen, John Patterson, Tony Smith, Dorothy Thompson,
Meg Thorpe and Julie Wilkinson.

Bob Lister, Director
Pat Story, Revision Editor
Roger Dalladay, Picture Editor

CONTENTS

Cambridge Latin Course Book II

Stage	Name	Cultural background	Main language features
13	**in Britanniā**	Life in Roman Britain: houses, mining, farming, slavery; career of Salvius.	Infinitive + **volō**, **nōlō**, **possum**. **-que**.
14	**apud Salvium**	The Romans in Britain: conquest, romanisation and trade, Boudica's rebellion.	Infinitive + **difficile**, **necesse**, etc. Agreement of adjectives in case and number. Form of adjectives: 1st, 2nd and 3rd declensions.
15	**rēx Cogidubnus**	Cogidubnus, king of the Regnenses, evidence for his reign.	Relative clauses. Imperfect tense of **possum**, **volō** and **nōlō**.
16	**in aulā**	The palace at Fishbourne.	Pluperfect tense. Relative clauses introduced by **quōs**, **quās**.
17	**Alexandrīa**	Roman Alexandria: growth of the city, trade, key buildings, racial tensions.	Genitive case.
18	**Eutychus et Clēmēns**	Glassmaking in Alexandria; government and economy of Egypt, peasant farmers.	Gender; agreement of adjectives and relative pronouns in gender.
19	**Īsis**	The worship of Isis: spring festival, initiation, spread of worship.	**hic** and **ille**. Imperative; **nōlī**, **nōlīte**. Vocative.
20	**medicus**	Alexandria: medicine, mathematics, astronomy, inventions.	Present participle. **is** and **ea** in accusative, genitive and dative.

INTRODUCTION

This book provides guidelines for teaching Stages 13–20 and information about the text and illustrations in the student's book. The aims and principles of the *Cambridge Latin Course*, teaching methods and the planning of the Course as a whole are explained in the Book I Teacher's Guide.

The content of Book II

The reading material is based as far as possible on historical characters and situations in two different parts of the Roman empire in the 1st century AD. Stages 13–16 are set in southern Britain, and Stages 17–20 in Alexandria. Continuity is provided by Quintus, son of Caecilius, who finds his way to Britain and there tells the story of his travels since his escape from the eruption of Vesuvius.

The characters in the stories are generally more realistic and sophisticated than the simple stereotypes in Book I. The increasing complexity of the language makes it easier to convey subtleties of character, motivation and atmosphere. There are many opportunities for students to go beyond the story line to examine the writer's intentions and to evaluate the evidence provided in the cultural background material and illustrations.

New language features continue to be introduced through model sentences. The students meet many examples of a feature in their reading before it is discussed and analysed. This experience is an important factor in enabling them to formulate their own rules with the teacher's help, rather than receive ready-made explanations.

Exercises both consolidate and test student recognition and understanding of a feature within the context of complete sentences. The level of difficulty increases towards the end of individual exercises, and as the Course proceeds. The stories also provide plentiful material for consolidation and practice of language features.

Each Stage contains suggestions for revision of paradigms and language features based on the 'Language information' at the end of Book II.

Supplementary exercises on the language and cultural background are available in the *Worksheet Masters* Book II, obtainable from Cambridge University Press; and in the *Independent Learning Manual* Book II, obtainable with the *Independent Learning Answer Book* from the Cambridge School Classics Project.

Consolidation and revision activities should not be tackled all at the same time. Plan to use a revision exercise at the start or end of several lessons. As in Book I, variety of activity and content are essential in every lesson.

Course planning

Advice is given in the Book I Teacher's Guide (pp. 10–12). For those moving quickly, some or all of the following stories and exercises may have to be omitted. They are marked ** in the Stage commentaries.

Stage 13 **Salvius fundum īnspicit** (p. 12)
Stage 14 **Domitilla cubiculum parat II** (p. 27)
　　　　　Quīntus advenit (p. 32)
Stage 15 **lūdī fūnebrēs I and II** (pp. 51–2)
Stage 17 **ad templum** (pp. 81–2)
Stage 18 **Clēmēns tabernārius** (pp. 98–9)
　　　　　Exercise 2 (p. 104)
Stage 19 **pompa** (pp. 119–20)
Stage 20 **fortūna crūdēlis** (pp. 136–7)
　　　　　Exercise 3 **Narcissus** (p. 141)

If a story has to be omitted, it is essential to give the students a summary of its content.

Assessment and feedback are important factors in student motivation and achievement. Detailed advice is given in the Book I Teacher's Guide (p. 19). Students should also be encouraged to assess their own progress by keeping a record of completed tasks and activities and marks gained.

STAGE 13 in Britanniā

Cultural background	Story line	Main language features	Focus of exercises
Life in Roman Britain: houses, mining, farming, slavery; career of Salvius.	The farm manager describes how his master Salvius has been injured while inspecting a mine. Salvius arrives home and vents his anger on his slaves.	• Infinitives. • volō, nōlō, possum. • -que.	1 Infinitive + volō, nōlō, possum. 2 Nominative singular and plural. 3 Perfect tense: 1st, 2nd and 3rd person singular.

Opening page (p. 1)

Illustration. Reconstruction of early Romano-British farmstead. To establish the context of Roman Britain, compare this homestead with the colourful town houses in Pompeii, and invite students to suggest reasons for the differences, e.g.: climate, local materials, remoteness from the centre of fashion, agricultural lifestyle. These simple British homesteads are discussed in the cultural background material (pp. 16–19). At this stage it is sufficient to note the timber frame, walls of wattle and daub, thatched roof, and entrance protected against the weather. The British costume is also adapted to local conditions: the man wears a dyed homespun tunic, hitched up for ease of movement over trousers, and the woman wears her plaid tunic long over an ankle-length skirt. Tools, garments and jewelry would be home produced. The moustache is based on the evidence of coins and sculpture (*Poole, Dorset, Upton Heritage Park. Photo G. Soffe*).

Model sentences (pp. 2–4)

New language feature. Infinitive with present tense of **volō** and **possum**. Allow students initially to translate **potest** by *is able*, in order to reinforce the infinitive, graduating to *can* by the end of the Stage.

New vocabulary. **cūrat** (new meaning), **potest, fessus, vult, vōcem, suāvem, agilis, saltāre, geminī, nōlunt**.

First reading. Aim to develop interest in the new characters before examining the language in detail. Establish the fact that Salvius is a wealthy Roman of high status. His wife Rufilla is wearing a very elaborate and expensive necklace. The slaves' jobs suggest their nationality and education: Varica, the British but romanised estate overseer, knowledgeable about local conditions; Philus, the educated Greek secretary; Volubilis, whose eyes betray his Egyptian origins; Bregans, the unromanised British labourer; the artistic twins bought by their sophisticated owners to provide home entertainment.

Illustrations. Philus' abacus in drawing 4 may be familiar to students with younger siblings. Abacuses are still used by market traders in the Middle East and Russia.

trēs servī (p. 5)

Story. The slaves' depression is lifted when the farm manager arrives with news that their master has been injured in a plot.

First reading. Elicit by questions the slaves' mood and the reasons for it. If necessary refer to the drawings on pp. 2–4 to identify individual slaves.

Consolidation. Dramatic reading of the story in Latin. A useful exercise to test accuracy occurs in *Independent Learning Manual* Stage 13.

Introduce the new format of the vocabulary: *verbs* are now listed as they occur in the story, followed by the infinitive and meaning; *nouns* are also listed as they occur, followed by the nominative singular and meaning.

Illustrations. Slave chains from Lord's Bridge, Cambridgeshire (left), and Anglesey (right). These illustrations make the point that slaves, particularly those working on large rural estates and in the mines, could be cruelly treated, and will serve as a 'trailer' for the next story, **coniūrātiō**.

coniūrātiō (p. 7)

Story. During his inspection of an iron mine, Salvius orders the death of a sick slave. The slave's son manages to enter Salvius' bedroom and wound him before being killed by the guards. Salvius demands that all the slaves should be put to death as a reprisal, but has to be content with the execution of the guards.

First reading. As an introduction, ask the students to recall from Book I objects found in Pompeii that were made of iron: storage chests, tools, razors, **stylī**, pots and pans, gladiatorial weapons. Britain's reputation for mineral wealth was one of the reasons for the Roman conquest, and it is likely that one of Salvius' duties was to maximise the benefits to the imperial government. There are useful comprehension questions in *Independent Learning Manual* Stage 13.

Discussion

1 Read the section on the career of Salvius on p. 21. Establish that he is a much more important figure than any of the characters the students have met so far in the Course. Ask students to refer to their reading when answering the question beneath the drawing. Does the fact that Salvius may have been pressurised by the emperor to increase the revenues from Britain make him a more sympathetic figure?

2   Is **coniūrātiō** a suitable title for the story? Does the title reflect the Roman paranoia about slave rebellions, especially in situations where the slaves were likely to feel desperate?

3   Discuss the rights of slaves and Roman justice. In Britain, at the edge of the empire, Roman officials were largely unsupervised and might be oppressive. Reinforce the discussion by a reading of **The slaves** in the background material (p. 20).

4   Generate suspense by asking how the three slaves would react to the news of Salvius' injury and his imminent homecoming.

Consolidation. Note the switch back to past tenses. *Worksheet Master* 13.1 offers a revision exercise on tenses.

Illustrations. Roman bloomery (smelting) site at Beauport Park, 5km from the coast at Hastings, East Sussex, the most extensive mine in the area. The tiles stamped CL BR (**classis Britannica**) are from a bath house on the site. Mining iron was arduous at every stage. Slave labour was used for: extracting the rock from the ground; manhandling the bellows to bring the furnaces to a temperature hot enough to purify the metal; hammering and re-heating the iron to refine it further; and transporting the iron pigs. The Roman fleet had a role rather like that of the Royal Engineers; it was responsible for road and bridge building and engineering of all kinds, including mining. Some small mines were privately owned and some were let out to private contractors.

Bregāns (pp. 8–9)

Story. Varica summons the slaves to parade for inspection. Bregans brings a hunting dog, a gift from King Cogidubnus. On his arrival Salvius is irritated by Bregans' attempts to draw his attention to the dog, and strikes him to the ground. The dog jumps at Salvius, who decides to punish Bregans instead of the dog.

First reading. Read the story aloud in Latin, and let the students explore it in groups before tackling the questions on p. 9 with the whole class. Keep up the pace to sustain interest in the new situation. Students could produce written answers for homework as consolidation of the oral discussion. Where the answer is a matter of opinion (questions 6, 11 and 12), any answer should be accepted which is a sensible interpretation of the situation and supported by reasons. The answers and mark scheme are as follows.

		Marks
1	The master/Salvius was arriving. Varica told the twins to call the slaves into the courtyard.	2
2	**celeriter cucurrērunt**. They were frightened of Salvius.	2

3 The slave-girls were getting a bedroom ready for their master.
   Volubilis was preparing the dinner.   2
4 King Cogidubnus had sent the dog for Salvius.   1
   The dog was very fierce; it could chase wild animals very
   well/it was a very good hunting dog.   2
5 Salvius was riding at the head of a large troop of horsemen.
   Accept 19 or 20 horsemen.   2
6 Salvius made no reply; he was furious.   2
   Bregans shouted out (instead of waiting to greet Salvius when
   he and Varica approached)/he used Salvius' name (instead of
   referring to him as **domine**).   1
7 He fell to the ground.   1
8 The dog broke away from the row and made for Salvius.   2
9 Some of the slaves.   1
   They broke away from the rows and dragged the dog back.   2
10 He wanted to kill the dog. Bregans told him that his friend,
   King Cogidubnus, had given him the dog.   2
11 *No:* he was eager to tell Salvius about the dog and meant no
   disrespect/it was not Bregans' fault that the dog broke free
   and attacked Salvius/he was trying to be helpful.
   Yes: Bregans should have had more sense than to alienate his
   cruel master/he should have had the dog under better
   control/he should not have brought the dog to the inspection
   in the first place/he shouldn't have made a smart comment.   1
12 *Brave:* he dared to answer Salvius back, thus saving the dog.
   Stupid: he should have had more sense than to anger his
   cruel master.
   Impetuous: he called out to Salvius when he should have
   kept silent.
   Cheeky: he should have addressed Salvius more respectfully.   2
                                                             TOTAL 25

Consolidation. This story is suitable for acting. It can also form a base,
when it has been read and discussed, for grammatical exercises, e.g.:
1 1st and 2nd person of the imperfect (introduced in Stage 12), by
   substitution for forms of the imperfect appearing in the story. Ask
   students the meaning of **ambulābat** (line 6), and then substitute with
   ambulābās, ambulābāmus, etc.
   Similarly with the perfect, ask for the meaning of **intrāvērunt** (line 18)
   and then substitute **intrāvistis**, etc.
2 Verbs with no nominative stated, taken in context, e.g.:
   vīlicus per ōrdinēs ambulābat; servōs **īnspiciēbat** et **numerābat** (lines 5–6).
   ubi sunt ancillae? nūllās ancillās **videō** (line 7).
   canis ferōcissimus est; bēstiās optimē **agitāre potest** (lines 16–17).

Bregantem ferōciter **pulsāvit** (lines 30–1).
istum canem **interficere volō** (line 35).

Illustration. Detail of hunting mosaic from Carthage, 5th century AD (*Tunis, Bardo Museum*). The dog is about to seize a hare. The image is reversed to suit the page.

About the language 1: infinitives (pp. 10–11)

New language feature. Present tense of **volō**, **nōlō**, **possum**, used with the infinitive.

Discussion. In paragraph 3, elicit from the students the comment that the endings of **possum** are the same as the forms of **sum**. In paragraph 5, ask for alternative translations of **possum** and encourage the most natural English version in each instance.

Consolidation. Students should learn to recognise and translate the inflections of the three verbs tabulated in paragraph 3. A useful oral exercise is to turn the examples in paragraphs 4 and 5 from singular to plural, or vice versa, and ask for a translation.

After studying the notes and the examples, ask different groups to look back at different stories, picking out and translating sentences containing infinitives. If further practice is necessary, ask the class Latin questions to which they can find the Latin answer in the text, e.g.: from **trēs servī** (p. 5)

Q quis ad Ītaliam redīre vult?   A Philus ad Ītaliam redīre vult.
Q quid Philus dīcit?   A ego ad Ītaliam redīre volō.

Illustration. Colour-coated hunt beaker made in the Nene valley near Peterborough. The quarry, a hare, is on the reverse. The animals and decorative swirls are made by trailing liquid clay onto the surface of the pot before firing (*By courtesy of Verulamium Museum, St Albans. Photo Jennifer Lowe*).

**Salvius fundum īnspicit (p. 12)

Story. Varica conducts Salvius around the farm. Seeing the ploughmen idle because the foreman is ill, Salvius wants to deny them food and sell the foreman. He is also annoyed because a new barn has collapsed when charged by a bull in the care of Bregans.

First reading. Divide the story into two or three parts. After reading part of the story aloud in Latin, allow the students time to explore it. Then check their understanding and interpretation with comprehension questions, e.g.:

What did Salvius want to do?
Who took him over the farm?
What did Varica say about the harvest?

What was stored in the granary?

What was the name of the slave in charge of the ploughmen?

Why was he absent?

What was the effect of his absence?

When Salvius proposed to get rid of him, how did Varica defend him?

Why did Salvius grudge the ploughmen their food?

What did Salvius see near the granary?

Why was it half-ruined?

Why did Salvius consider Bregans **stultior quam cēterī**?

What impression do you get of Salvius as an estate owner?

Discussion. The reading of this story should be combined with a discussion of farming and slavery in Roman Britain (pp. 16–20).

1   *Salvius as an estate owner.* What impression do we receive of his involvement and efficiency? He has a manager, but takes a personal interest in the farm. His impersonal approach to slaves would be regarded as normal, and is based on Cato's advice to a landowner in *De Agri Cultura* II.

2   *Varica's character.* Is he the right kind of person to be farm manager?

3   *The conditions of farm slaves.* Why was the life of farm slaves generally much worse than that of domestic slaves? Give examples from the lives of slaves encountered in this Stage and Book I.

Illustration. Wall-painting from Trier showing Gallo-Roman farmhouse consisting of two blocks joined by a colonnade. The master, wearing his hooded travelling cloak (left), arrives home to be greeted by his slaves.

About the language 2: -que (p. 13)

New language feature. Use of **-que** to link words and sentences.

Discussion. Emphasise the unchanging form of **-que**, to avoid future confusion with the relative pronoun. After studying paragraph 2, put up sentences on the board for students to rewrite using **-que**, e.g.:

Vārica dominum salūtāvit et fundum ostendit.

Salvius agrōs circumspectāvit et arātōrēs quaesīvit.

Salvius ad horreum advēnit et aedificium sēmirutum cōnspexit.

Consolidation. Oral practice of **-que** linking two words can provide useful vocabulary revision. There is a further exercise in *Independent Learning Manual* Stage 13.

Practising the language (pp. 14–15)

Exercise 1. Complete the sentences by selecting an appropriate infinitive.

Exercise 2. Complete the sentences by selecting a correct nominative, singular or plural.

Exercise 3. A short reading passage with gaps, to be completed by selection of verb in correct person of perfect tense. This exercise may be taken orally. Insist that each verb is translated in the context of the sentence as a whole. Encourage students to re-order the words in their translation, to produce the most natural English, e.g.:

Because the slave was tired, he … (line 1)
After Salvius entered the bedroom, he … (line 3).

See 'Language information', p. 167, for similar examples.

Illustrations. Scenes from rural life: man milking goat (p. 14), one man and his dog (p. 15). Details of mosaic from Daphne, suburb of Antioch, *c.* AD 325 (*Louvre*).

Language information: revision

Revise the present, imperfect and perfect tenses (p. 160). Use exercises 1 and 2 (p. 161, top) and further examples at the start or end of lessons so that the reinforcement value is increased. Leave exercise 3 for later revision since it contains the pluperfect introduced in Stage 16. See also *Worksheet Masters* 13.1 and *Independent Learning Manual* Stage 13.

Cultural background material (pp. 16–21)

Content. Life in Roman Britain: houses, mining, farming, slavery; the career of Salvius. Study of this material should be integrated with reading and language work, as suggested earlier.

Discussion

1   *Houses.* By studying the illustrations trace the change from roundhouse (pp. 16–17) to rectangular house (p. 1 and the plan on p. 17) to the simple corridor house (p. 18) to the rich man's elaborate villa of the fourth century AD (p. 17). Salvius' villa would have been more elaborate than the corridor house on p. 18, but simpler than those of later centuries (p. 17). Stress the point that the coming of the Romans probably made little difference to the great majority of peasant farmers, who continued to live in round or simple rectangular houses.

2   *Agriculture.* The Romans introduced few changes in farming practice. In pre-Roman times the Britons had increased their yields and were producing surpluses to market. There were further improvements in the Roman period because of the introduction of more efficient iron tools, which meant that more land could be cultivated. It was also easier to market produce because of Roman road building and the growth of towns.

3   *The status and working conditions of slaves.* These varied considerably, from the household where some would have a close relationship with their master, to the estate or mine where they worked in chain-gangs

under the control of a manager or overseer. The economy of the Roman empire depended on slave labour. Ever since the near-success of the revolt of Celtic, German and Thracian slaves under Spartacus in 73–71 BC, the Romans lived in constant fear of another uprising, and insubordination was met by the severest penalties.

4 *Salvius' character and career.* Salvius' career shows that he was successful and ambitious. Do the fictional stories in this Stage reinforce this? Do they reveal other characteristics?

Illustrations

p. 16 • Bronze horse harness mount (79mm) from East Anglia, with red enamel decoration and swirling abstract patterns typical of Celtic taste (*Photo courtesy of University of Cambridge Museum of Archaeology and Anthropology*).

• Reconstructed roundhouses and detail of wattle and daub, Butser Experimental Ancient Farm, near Petersfield, Hampshire.

p. 17 • Inside a roundhouse. Status is demonstrated by well-crafted objects rather than the functional architectural style. The entrance usually faced south-east to make the best of the morning sun and offer protection against cold north winds. Separate rooms for different purposes, e.g. bedrooms, could have been made by hanging leather or cloth between the uprights and the outer wall. The smoke from the fire would serve a useful purpose in smoking joints of meat and keeping down vermin in the thatch. If well-seasoned wood was burned on the hearth the amount of smoke would have been tolerable (*Photo Simon James*).

• After *Roman Villas and the Countryside* by Bédoyère (*English Heritage*). As shown by the broken line, the roundhouse has not been completely excavated.

• Drawing by Alan Sorrell of Lullingstone Roman villa as it may have appeared in AD 360. At top centre is a temple-mausoleum, at top right a round temple. Salvius' villa is imagined as that at Angmering near Worthing (now covered up) which excavation showed to be unusually elaborate for the 1st century, with planning and craftsmanship only surpassed at Fishbourne.

p. 18 • Sheep at Butser. The Soay breed, found feral in the Outer Hebrides, has a bone structure identical with Iron Age archaeological findings. The bones on Roman sites relate to Shetland sheep. Shears first appear in the Roman period.

• Reconstruction of villa near Verulamium, with thatched roof and tiled verandah. The lower walls are of stone, the upper of wattle and daub. Note: ploughing with a yoke of oxen, cabbages (highly valued by the Romans), chickens, cattle in pen, beehives in wood, timber-felling, watering sheep at well.

p. 19 • Plough-team, 5cm high, 2nd–3rd century AD, found at Magis (Piercebridge), County Durham (*British Museum*). The yoked beasts pull forward a beam jointed just above soil level to a sickle-shaped sole with an iron tip. This the man steers straight with his left hand, pushing it downwards with even pressure into the soil, while goading his oxen forward with his right.

• Emmer. The protein value of ancient wheat was about twice that of most modern cereals. Cato (*De Agri Cultura*, LVI–LVII) recommends as the ration for chain-gang slaves 2kg of bread a day in winter, 2.5kg when they were digging the vines, but 2kg again when the figs ripened. Ten amphorae of wine per man a year (about 20l a month), presumably mixed with water, was reasonable (for pictures of amphorae, see model sentences to Stage 14 and note in *Independent Learning Manual* Stage 14). Cato recommended that sick slaves had their rations reduced.

• Coin minted in Camulodunum by Cunobelin, king of the Catuvellauni (d. AD 41), with CVN and horse on other side (*British Museum*). Under Claudius the Romans took over his tribal stronghold at Colchester as their first provincial capital, later transferring to London.

p. 20 • Bronze oil flask, 9cm high, 2nd century AD, from Isurium Brigantium (Aldborough), Yorkshire (*British Museum*). The slave-boy sits in his cloak, a lantern (probably) between his legs.

p. 22 • Rich torcs were commonly worn into battle by warrior chieftains. They illustrate the high level of craftsmanship among the Britons, and the emphasis placed on portable wealth and status symbols. One of twelve *c.* 70 BC found in Snettisham, Norfolk.

Suggested activities

1 Writing, based on what students have read, e.g.: a story about a slave transferred from a farm to a mine; or a group play about slaves' everyday life in a British villa or a conversation about Salvius between two friends, one who admires him and one who dislikes him.

2 Exercises on British and Roman farming in *Independent Learning Manual* Stage 13 and *Worksheet Masters* 13.3 and 13.5.

3 Study of a local villa.

Vocabulary checklist (p. 22)

Discuss the format used in the vocabulary checklists from now on: *verbs* in 1st person singular present, present infinitive, 1st person singular perfect; *nouns* in nominative (the genitive is added in Stage 17).

STAGE 14 apud Salvium

Cultural background	Story line	Main language features	Focus of exercises
The Romans in Britain: conquest, romanisation and trade, Boudica's rebellion.	As Rufilla plans to entertain a visitor, the maid cajoles the cook into doing her work, and Salvius is annoyed to find his study furniture moved to the guest room. The visitor turns out to be Quintus. Invited to visit King Cogidubnus, Salvius searches in vain for a gift as splendid as Quintus'.	• Infinitive + **difficile**, **necesse**, etc. • Agreement of adjectives in case and number. • Form of adjectives: 1st, 2nd and 3rd declensions.	1 Agreement of adjectives. 2 Imperfect tense of **esse**.

Opening page (p. 23)

apud may be introduced to students learning French by reference to *chez* as in *chez Sylvie, chez moi.*

Illustration. Reconstruction of Romano-British room (*Museum of London*), since remodelled. The pottery is authentic, and the cupboard is based on a relief showing items for use by the dead in the next world, from inside a Romano-German sarcophagus. Red and black decor was high-status decoration in Herculaneum, so the room aspires to Roman elegance even in Britain. Reserve discussion of the picture until **Rūfilla** (p. 25) is read.

Model sentences (p. 24)

New language features. Infinitive with **difficile est** and **necesse est**. This extension of the use of the infinitive causes few problems.

   Imperative plural. The singular was introduced in Stage 10. The language note on the imperative does not occur until Stage 19, p. 121. Comment at this stage is generally unnecessary since the context makes the meaning absolutely clear.

New vocabulary. gravis, necesse.

First reading. The translation is usually straightforward. If students experience difficulty with any feature, give them further examples.

Discussion. Varica's difficulty in establishing his authority with his fellow-slaves, and the attitude of Bregans the Briton.

Consolidation. Re-read dramatically in groups of four to establish as a unit infinitive + **difficile** and **necesse est.**

Rūfilla (p. 25)

Story. Rufilla complains of her life on a country estate in winter, far from London and her friends. Salvius reminds her that she chose the house herself and has the benefits of a large household.

First reading. Set the scene by studying the illustration on p. 23. After a lively Latin reading, groups could be asked to prepare the speeches of Rufilla or Salvius for dramatic reading, initially in English, then in Latin.

Discussion

1 *Rufilla* should not be casually dismissed as a nagging wife. Her name Vitellia suggests that she came from an old family of the Roman nobility, probably with a number of country estates in the most beautiful parts of Italy as well as a town house in Rome. As the wife of Salvius she would have been courted as a central figure in society when she arrived in London.

2 *Domestic slaves.* The number, tasks and status of the various slaves can be noted from this and following stories. Ask the students why Rufilla sent her **ōrnātrīcēs** from the room before arguing with Salvius.

3 *London* was probably by this time, about AD 81, the administrative centre of Britain. By making his base in London, Salvius would have had good communications with Rome and other parts of Britain, as well as access to imported luxuries.

Consolidation. A useful story for revising verbs in different tenses and persons in context.

Illustration. Ornate comb, probably made of bone, likely to have belonged to a wealthy, fashionable woman; and manicure set including nail cleaners, cosmetic scoops and (at right) tweezers (*Museum of London*).

Domitilla cubiculum parat I (pp. 26–7)

Story. Domitilla, a hairdresser, resents being ordered to sweep the guest bedroom. Her tears prompt the cook to do it for her, and she rewards him with a kiss.

First reading. Take the story quickly, perhaps leading the class through it with comprehension questions, inviting more precise translation of verbs or sentences which you wish them to notice, e.g.:

necesse est nōbīs cubiculum parāre (line 3).
necesse est tibi cubiculum verrere (line 7).
cubiculum verrere nōlēbat (line 10).
nōn decōrum est ōrnātrīcibus cubiculum verrere (lines 11–12).
necesse est mihi cubiculum parāre (lines 17–18).
nōn diūtius labōrāre possum (line 18).

Treat **nōlī lacrimāre** as a vocabulary item at this point. More examples will be introduced before the discussion on p. 121.

Illustration. Ostentation on a family tomb. Note the distribution of tasks between the ornatrices when dressing and making up their mistress: front hair, back hair, holding the mirror, holding a jug. Basketwork chairs were popular with Roman ladies (*Trier, Rheinisches Landesmuseum*).

**Domitilla cubiculum parat II (p. 27)

Story. Domitilla gets the old slave-woman Marcia to wash the floor, then hurries to her mistress to gain credit. Rufilla praises the cleaning but laments the plainness of the room. Domitilla helpfully or mischievously reminds her of the luxurious furniture in Salvius' study.

First reading. Students may still need help to translate in a natural English order those sentences with embedded subordinate clauses, e.g.:

Domitilla, ubi … clāmāvit (lines 2–3).
Marcia, quamquam … dīxit (line 6).
sed, quamquam … dormīre (lines 12–14).

Discussion. The irony of the title; Domitilla's status as an ornatrix, her character and her attitude to Marcia, Volubilis and Rufilla.

Consolidation. Oral practice of phrases containing the infinitive.

About the language 1: adjectives (pp. 28–9)

New language feature. Adjectives: function, agreement (case and number) and position. Adjectives are introduced step-by-step. The later steps, which should not be anticipated, are:

agreement of adjectives of a different declension from the noun (p. 31);
agreement of adjectives by gender (Stage 18, p. 100).

Discussion. In paragraphs 3 and 5, if students are having difficulty with the technical terms, help them to approach the pairing by asking questions about the meaning: *Who* was frightened? *Who* was good? *Who* were happy?

Consolidation. It is a good idea to return to this note briefly in several consecutive lessons, asking the students to translate and explain the examples, so that these become sufficiently familiar to be a point of reference if difficulties arise later.

Illustration. Guilloche border to mosaic floor, very common in Britain.

in tablīnō (p. 30)

Story. Rufilla finds Salvius annoyed about his missing furniture, especially as Quintus, now revealed as the unexpected guest, comes from Pompeii, whose citizens Salvius mistrusts.

First reading. Possible comprehension questions:

What does Salvius have to do?
Why does Rufilla address him as **mī Salvī** and **mī cārissime**?

What mood is Salvius in? Why?

Why is Salvius not able to find his chair and cupboard? What else is missing from the study?

Why is Rufilla pleased about Quintus' visit? Why does Salvius not like the idea?

Discussion. Allow the answers to lead into a discussion of motivation and character. Rufilla exaggerates Quintus' social standing in calling him **vir nōbilis** (line 28), since his grandfather was a freedman. Salvius' annoyance betrays him into an outburst of prejudice against profiteering Pompeians.

Consolidation. A dramatic reading by volunteers or in pairs or rows. First ensure students have an accurate understanding of the text by:

1 vocabulary revision, e.g.: **celeriter, cōnficere, aliquid, nunc, cēpit, dēlēvit, probī, dēcipiēbant**, etc.

2 practice of linguistic features, e.g.: **commodum/decōrum est** + infinitive, **num, volō/nōlō** + infinitive, **mendāciōrēs quam, sellam armāriumque**, etc.

About the language 2: more about adjectives (p. 31)

New language feature. Agreement of adjectives and nouns of different declensions.

Discussion. Work straight through paragraphs 1–3, using the simple language of the students' text, i.e. 'the endings do not look the same'. If students show anxiety or confusion, point out that they have already handled successfully several examples of adjectives which agree with their nouns although the endings do not look the same, e.g. model sentences 2 and 3, **amphora gravis, amphoram gravem**, etc.

Consolidation. Look back at the previous examples in the stories, and ask the students to identify the noun the adjective is describing, and the case and number of each noun and adjective pair, e.g.:

Page 25: urbs pulcherrima (line 6), duās ōrnātrīcēs (line 23).

Page 27: urnam gravem (line 2), familiārī meō (line 13).

Page 30: mercātōrēs Pompēiānī (line 25), familiāris meus (line 27), vir nōbilis (line 28), familiārem meum (line 31).

Illustration. Outer surface of wax tablet found in the Walbrook stream, London, branded with PROC AVG DEDERVNT BRIT PROV, meaning 'issued by the imperial procurators (civilian administrators) of Britain' (*British Museum*).

**Quīntus advenit (p. 32)

Story. Quintus is greeted politely by Salvius. He compliments Rufilla on the meal and comments on the elegance of his bedroom; Salvius ironically agrees.

First reading. This story should be taken at one reading.

Discussion topic. Is Salvius' manner hypocritical, or is he showing politeness to a guest, or civility to a man with the status of Roman citizen? What can we learn about Rufilla's character from her comments to Quintus?

Consolidation. The comprehension questions could be set for homework, following the class discussion. The answers and the mark scheme are as follows. Give credit for any sensible answer.

Marks

1 *Four remarks and four explanations from the following:*   8
   Salvius says:
   'You are very welcome.' On the contrary, Salvius did not trust Pompeians and was horrified that Quintus had been invited.
   'We have prepared a very good bedroom for you.' It was Rufilla who prepared the bedroom.
   'Wasn't that a terrible disaster?' In fact Salvius may have welcomed it since he disliked the Pompeians.
   Rufilla says:
   'I have prepared a modest dinner for you.' The description she gives of it suggests the opposite.
   'The bedroom is not elaborately furnished,' etc. In fact she has imported some elegant furniture from Salvius' study.

2 **Two of:** Quintus does not seem to be able to get a word in edgeways/he may have been tired from his journey/unwilling to talk about the tragedy that has befallen him/he senses the tension between Salvius and Rufilla and keeps quiet.   2

TOTAL 10

Illustration. Oysters and other shellfish were a popular delicacy. Shown with Romano-British dish and spoon (*St Albans, Verulamium Museum*).

tripodes argenteī (pp. 33–4)

Story. In preparation for a visit to King Cogidubnus, Quintus selects two silver tripods as a gift. Salvius tries to outdo him, but can find nothing better than an antique bronze urn.

First reading. Plan to handle this story quickly, perhaps asking the students to prepare it in advance and checking their understanding with comprehension questions, e.g.:
   Who came into the bedroom to speak to Quintus?
   What message did he bring?
   Who was to be honoured that day? Why?
   What gift did Quintus have in his box and for whom was it intended?

Why do you think Salvius said 'no' to his steward's first two suggestions?
Why did the steward discourage Salvius from taking the **statua aurāta**?
Suggest a suitable translation for the last sentence.
Do you think Salvius had originally intended to take a present to Cogidubnus?
What reasons do you think Salvius had for offering a present to the king?

Consolidation. Divide the class into groups of four; ask them to allocate the parts and re-read or act the play.

Discussion

1 *Relations with King Cogidubnus.* Read the sections on British tribal chieftains and the Roman conquest (pp. 36–7 and p. 41). In recognition of his co-operation, Cogidubnus was allowed to rule his tribe, the Regnenses, as a client king. (This is discussed in detail in Stage 15, pp. 55–6.) As the representative of the emperor, Salvius would be careful to lend Cogidubnus public support and respect, and Cogidubnus would defer to Salvius.

2 *Value of metals.* Cheapest is something made of bronze (**aēneus**), more expensive something made of silver (**argenteus**), most valuable something made of gold (**aureus**). In considering a gold-plated (**aurātus**) present, Salvius would be offering something that appeared good but had relatively little value. Does this shed any light on his character?

3 *Imported goods.* Introduce the background information about British imports and exports (pp. 37–8 and p. 40).

Illustrations

- Tripods and jug. Tripods were often fitted with a tray or bowl at the top and were frequently used in religious ceremonies to make offerings of food and wine to the gods or to burn incense.
- One of seven cups from the Hockwold treasure, Norfolk, 1st century AD (*British Museum*), showing that good-quality Roman silver was in use in Britain at the time of Salvius.

Practising the language (p. 35)

Exercise 1. Complete the sentences by selecting an adjective to agree with the noun. This consolidates both language notes in this Stage. Additional exercises can be found in *Independent Learning Manual* Stage 14 and *Worksheet Masters* 14.2 and 14.3.

Exercise 2. Complete the sentences with the appropriate person of **eram**, which was introduced in Book I, Stage 12. Students may need to be reminded of the meaning.

Language information: revision

Nouns in 1st, 2nd and 3rd declensions: draw up and discuss a table showing the nominative, accusative and dative, singular and plural, of **puella**, **servus**, **mercātor**, **leō** and **cīvis**, before asking the students to attempt the examples in paragraphs 5 and 6 on p. 151. The genitive is not introduced until Stage 17 and should not be discussed before then.

Cultural background material (pp. 36–41)

Content. British tribal system, invasions of Caesar and Claudius, romanisation and trade, Boudica's revolt. Against this background the students begin to appreciate Salvius' work and position; the events at Cogidubnus' palace in Stages 15–16; and the wider picture of Roman Britain under Agricola which is developed in Book III.

Discussion. Break up this long section by reading part of it after **tripodes argenteī**. The section on Boudica can conveniently be read after 'Practising the language' or the revision exercises in 'Language information'. Suitable questions on pp. 36–40 are:

Why did the Romans want to invade Britain?

Why did they find Britain difficult to conquer?

By what methods did they achieve success?

What were the advantages and disadvantages of living within the Roman empire?

Why did Boudica fascinate the Romans?

The chart of important events and dates (p. 41) can be used for quick revision now or later. Use the pictures as a basis for questions, such as:

Why are the three emperors whose portraits appear here particularly important in the history of Britain?

What message is the coin meant to convey?

Whom does the sculpture commemorate? Why do you think it was made?

What does the bottom picture show?

The picture of the model of Fishbourne palace provides a useful 'trailer' for the next Stage.

Illustrations

p. 36 • Skull of Iron Age warrior, Deal, Kent, 3rd century BC (*British Museum*), buried with an iron sword, with decorated scabbard and belt fitting; an ornate brooch; and a decorated bronze crown indicating high status.

• Statue heads of Julius Caesar, and Claudius wearing honorary wreath (*Naples Archaeological Museum*).

p. 37 • Lindow Man, a body found in the peat of Lindow Moss, Cheshire (*British Museum*), reconstructed in wax by Richard Neave. A man of fine physique aged 25, likely to have been of high status because his fingernails were undamaged by manual work. He was sacrificed by the triple death (hit on the head, garrotted, throat cut) according to Celtic ritual, and thrown in the marsh as a sacrifice to the Celtic gods, possibly to avert the Roman invaders.

- Richborough may have been the landing place of Claudius' invasion force.
- Aureus (gold coin), minted to celebrate the dedication of Claudius' triumphal arch in AD 52, showing the arch with Claudius on horseback, two trophies and DE BRITANN[IS] (*British Museum*).
- The inscription from Claudius' arch has been reconstructed by comparison with honorific dedications to other emperors in comparable circumstances. Cogidubnus was probably one of the eleven kings.

[ ] = missing part of stone; ( ) = expansion of abbreviation.

TI(BERIO) CLAV[DIO DRVSI F(ILIO) CAI]SARI
AVGV[STO GERMANI]CO
PONTIFIC[I MAXIMO TRIB(VNICIA) POTES]TAT(E) XI
CO(N)S(VL) V IM[PERATORI XII PATRI PA]TRIAI
SENATVS PO[PVLVSQUE] RO[MANVS Q]VOD
REGES BRIT[ANNIAE] XI [DEVICTOS SINE]
VLLA IACTV[RA IN DEDITIONEM ACCEPERIT]
GENTESQVE B[ARBARAS TRANS OCEANVM]
PRIMVS IN DICI[ONEM POPVLI ROMANI REDEGERIT]

To Tiberius Claudius, son of Drusus, Caesar
Augustus Germanicus,
Pontifex Maximus, holding tribune's powers for the eleventh time,
consul for the fifth time, hailed Imperator twelve times, Father of his country –
the Senate and People of Rome [dedicate this monument] because
eleven British kings, defeated without
any loss, he received in subjection,
and the barbarian races on the other side of the sea
he first brought under the rule of the Roman people.

p. 38
- Watling Street passing through Northamptonshire (see map, p. 40).
- Reconstruction of temple of Claudius from Colchester, a **colōnia** of veterans. It was possibly the most imposing building in Britain until destroyed by Boudica. The substructure survives as the foundations of the Norman castle (*Colchester Castle Museum*).
- Boudica and her daughters sculpted by Thomas Thornycroft, seen as a symbol of the expansion of British power under Victoria.

p. 39
- Victim of Boudica's sack of London, from Walbrook (*Museum of London*).

- Burnt dates and one plum found with fragments of charred fabric in building destroyed in Boudica's sack of Colchester (*Colchester Castle Museum*).
- Life-size bronze head of Claudius from River Alde, Saxmundham, Suffolk (*British Museum*). The jagged edges show it was torn from a full-length statue.
- Samian ware from government store or shop, deliberately smashed before the building was fired by Boudica. The red pottery has burned black in places (*Colchester Castle Museum*).

p. 40
- Relief of lead miner, possibly Roman, holding pick and bucket to transport ore (*Wirksworth Church, Derbyshire*).
- Reconstruction of burial of Briton, late 1st century BC, Welwyn Garden City, Hertfordshire (*British Museum*). It contained a Roman silver wine cup, evidence of trade after Caesar's invasion but before the Claudian settlement.

p. 41
- The illustrations are all annotated elsewhere in text. Left: Claudius (p. 36), Vespasian (p. 57); right: Julius Caesar (p. 36), aureus of Claudius (p. 37), Boudica (p. 38), Fishbourne palace (p. 69), eruption of Vesuvius (Book I, p. 161).

p. 42
- Detail from tombstone of Longinus Sdapeze, officer of 1st squadron of Thracian cavalry from Bulgaria (*Colchester Castle Museum*). Spiky hair of victim possibly stiffened with lime.

Suggested activities

1   Imagine you are Salvius and have been in Britain for six months. Write your first report to the emperor, selecting topics you think he will find interesting. Possibilities include: the British way of life and attitude to the Romans, agriculture and industries useful to the Romans, the morale of Roman officials and their families sent to Britain on duty.
2   Write a letter from Rufilla to a friend in Rome, describing her life, her British country villa and her occasional visits to London.
3   Other activities are suggested in *Independent Learning Manual* Stage 14, and *Worksheet Masters* 14.5 and 15.1.

Vocabulary checklist

num, like **nōnne**, is treated as a vocabulary item only and no further explanation is given. An exercise is provided in *Worksheet Master* 15.5 for use in Stage 15.

STAGE 15 rēx Cogidubnus

Cultural background	Story line	Main language features	Focus of exercises
Cogidubnus, king of the Regnenses, evidence for his reign.	Annoyed by crowds on the way to the palace, Salvius has two Britons and their cart thrown into the ditch. He and Quintus attend a ceremony and games in honour of Claudius. The Cantici win the athletic events but the Regnenses win the boat race.	• Relative clauses. • Imperfect tense of **possum**, **volō**, **nōlō**.	1 Accusative and dative case. 2 Phrases and verbs with the infinitive.

Opening page (p. 43)

Illustration. Detail from dedicatory inscription of temple to Neptune and Minerva, Chichester, now built into the outside wall of the Assembly Rooms. Note the excellence and proportion of the lettering, comparable with anything in Rome. In line 3 is part of the king's name. Tacitus called him Cogidubnus (see p. 31 of this Guide); modern scholars make a convincing case for Togidubnus (see p. 92 under R.S.O. Tomlin). The illustration is best discussed with the story **caerimōnia** (p. 48) and the background material (pp. 55–6).

Model sentences (pp. 44–5)

New language feature. Relative clauses, introduced by relative pronouns in the nominative and accusative singular (extended to nominative plural in stories).

New vocabulary. scēptrum, **diadēma**, **rēgīna**, **paterā**, **agnum**, **āram**, **victima**, **sacerdōs**, **bālāvit**.

First reading. Read sentences aloud in Latin with appropriate pauses and word grouping. Given this help the students will translate without difficulty, especially if they have met *qui* and *que* in French. Should problems arise, write the relative clause up as a sentence, e.g. **ancillae vīnum ferēbant**, with the students' translation underneath. Then return to the model sentence, and ask for a re-translation.

In sentences 4–6, students may need to discuss animal sacrifice (see notes on **caerimōnia** below) before they can concentrate on the language.

Consolidation. Return briefly to the model sentences in several subsequent lessons. This makes them sufficiently familiar to provide a point of reference later, when further developments arise. Postpone discussion until the language note.

Illustrations. The appearance of Cogidubnus, who is wearing a Roman toga and a Celtic gold circlet of high status, indicates the ambiguity of his position as a client king.

ad aulam (pp. 46–7)

Story. Riding in procession with Quintus to the palace, Salvius orders Varica to clear a route through the crowd. When his men force two young Britons and their cart into the ditch, Salvius laughs with satisfaction.

First reading. After reading the first paragraph in Latin, check the students' understanding by asking them to sketch the procession or present it diagrammatically, with people and objects in correct sequence and labelled in English or Latin.

Then divide the class into groups, asking each to prepare a translation of the speeches of one of the characters. When the class goes through the whole story, a comparison of different groups' translations will provoke illuminating discussion of the language. Afterwards there could be a dramatic reading by the whole class.

Discussion. Ask the class to identify the ways in which Salvius' rank, wealth and importance (his **dignitās**) are displayed, e.g.: his horse, outriders to clear the way, large retinue, the gifts they bear, his contemptuous attitude to the provincials.

Consolidation. The first paragraphs are useful for revising the imperfect tense, e.g.

What was the meaning of **agmen ad aulam prōcēdēbat** (line 1)?
What would **Salvius ad aulam prōcēdēbat** mean?
And **omnēs prōcēdēbant**?
And **prōcēdēbam**?
What was the meaning of **magna turba erat in viā** (lines 7–8)?
What would **erant in viā** mean?
And **in viā erāmus**?
What would be the Latin for *I was in the road*?
Refer if necessary to 'Language information' (pp. 160 and 162).

Illustration. Reconstruction of Cogidubnus' palace from the east (see p. 69).

caerimōnia (pp. 48–9)

Story. In a mixed gathering of Britons and Romans, Salvius and Quintus watch as the king makes a sacrifice, and a wax effigy of the Emperor

Claudius is placed on a pyre and burnt in a symbolic ceremony which frees an eagle to fly to heaven.

First reading. Set the scene by asking students why Salvius and Quintus have been invited to the palace. This was explained in **tripodes argenteī** (p. 33, lines 6–11).

Read the story aloud in Latin with appropriate pauses and expression, and encourage the shared translation of difficult sentences before the class tackles the comprehension questions, possibly orally in pairs. Written answers could be set for homework. The answers and mark scheme are as follows. Give credit for any sensible answer.

		Marks
1	In the atrium. British chieftains, women, Romans.	2
2	Large, noisy.	2
3	In the middle of the atrium, on a couch.	1
	The Emperor Claudius.	1
4	It was made by highly skilled craftsmen from Italy.	2
5	The crowd standing near the door fell to the ground.	2
	The British chieftains got up.	1
	The Romans were silent.	1
6	The king was lame.	1
7	Wine, (snow-white) lamb.	2
	The priests led the victims to the king (so that he could inspect them).	1
8	They lifted the couch on their shoulders and carried the image out of the atrium.	2
9	In the courtyard, on a pyre.	1
10	He put it into the pyre; the wax melted.	2
11	An eagle suddenly flew out of the image.	1
12	'The gods are summoning Claudius. His spirit is rising to the gods.'	2
	The eagle represented the soul of Claudius.	1
	TOTAL	25

Discussion

1 *Claudius.* Cogidubnus became a **cliēns** of Claudius during or soon after the invasion of Britain in AD 43. Claudius died in AD 54 and this story is set in AD 81, showing the steadfast loyalty of Cogidubnus to his patron, and the extent to which he is now living in the past. He does not recognise that, with the coming of Salvius, his position and prestige are almost ended.

2 *Sacrificial rituals.* It was a Roman custom to offer food and wine to the dead at their tombs on the anniversary of their birth, to reinvigorate them in the Underworld. Important public events were marked by

animal sacrifices to win the support of the gods. The animal was first stunned by a blow, then its throat was cut, the blood collected, the internal organs burned on the altar, and the meat cooked and eaten. If the future was in doubt, the priest would read the omens revealed by the condition of the liver.

3 *Aquila*. The eagle was the universal symbol of Roman power.

4 *Apotheosis*. This scene is based on the ritual for promoting an emperor to divinity after his death. Since the death of Augustus, the emperor's funeral pyre had a wax image on the top, from which an eagle was released. The effect was impressive, and the Romans liked magic tricks (cf. Stage 16 model sentences).

Consolidation. A good passage for identifying instances of the perfect tense, and practising manipulation in the same way as suggested for verbs in **ad aulam** (above), in readiness for the introduction of the pluperfect tense in the next Stage.

Illustration. A funeral pyre was rectangular, with the logs piled alternate ways, sometimes interwoven with papyrus to facilitate burning.

About the language 1: relative clauses (p. 50)

New language feature. Relative clauses describing the subject of the sentence.

Discussion. Students should work straight through p. 50 with your help. The aim is to enable them to:

recognise a relative clause,
identify the noun to which it refers,
translate it correctly.

There is no need at this point to analyse the relative pronouns. The immediate priority is to recognise and translate relative clauses correctly. At some point put on the board examples of English and Latin sentences containing relative pronouns and let students themselves spot parallels between initial *wh* in *who, which, when* and initial **qu** in **qui, quae, quem**, etc.

If a student enquires about **quod**, it is sufficient to say that the word has two meanings, *which* and *because*, and the appropriate choice is made according to the sense of the sentence. Show how the examples in **ad aulam** (p. 46, lines 5, 10 and 15) are unambiguous.

Consolidation. Return to the model sentences, or one of the earlier stories, and ask each student to find a sentence containing a relative clause, and

write out the sentence,
underline the relative clause,
ring the noun it describes,
translate the sentence.

This is a useful exercise for the student to keep and use for future revision.

There are further exercises in *Worksheet Master* 15.2 and *Independent Learning Manual* Stage 15.

lūdī fūnebrēs I and II (pp. 51–2)

Story. Cogidubnus leads his guests to the shore for the funeral games. The Cantici excel in the athletic contests, but in the boat race they are wrecked through the over-confidence of their captain, while the Regnenses return safely.

First reading. This story contains new vocabulary and unfamiliar concepts, and will need careful planning. Aim to read it at one sitting to maintain interest and momentum, keeping control in your own hands and breaking the story down for handling in different ways.

1 **post caerimōniam … ēmīsit** (lines 1–7): Read aloud and ask comprehension questions.

2 **postrēmō … intentē exspectābant** (lines 8–13): As you read the Latin get a student to tabulate on the board, with the class's help, the names of the tribes, the captains and their characters. Ask the students to foretell the winner and to keep to their affiliation.

3 **subitō tuba … ad mētam ruēbant** (p. 51, line 13 – p. 52, line 2): As the class give you the meaning, ask another student to draw a simple plan of the situation on the board, showing the shore and the rock. Emphasise the incompleteness of the imperfect **ruēbant**, heightening the suspense.

4 **nāvis Rēgnēnsis … mētae appropinquāvērunt** (lines 2–14): Read the Latin aloud sentence by sentence to keep up the pace, asking comprehension questions as you go. Invite volunteers from the appropriate team to translate or summarise the speeches. A representative could plot the movement of each group's boat on the board. Encourage the two groups to become involved, cheering and groaning as appropriate.

5 **Belimicus, quī … summersa erat** (lines 14–18): Ask the class to close their books and listen. Read the Latin aloud and pause at the end of each sentence to ask for a translation. Repeat if necessary with appropriate questions to help the class arrive at the meaning.

6 **intereā … Canticī miserī erant** (lines 19–22): Class translation. Ask the students which they consider the key word in this passage. Suggestions may include **cūrā, incolumis, pervēnit, laetī**. Any choice is acceptable as long as it is supported by sound reasons. Ascertain the majority view.

7 **tum omnēs … auxilium postulābat** (line 22–end): Ask the class what the last four lines add to the story, and let them work out the meaning in pairs. Some may consider the story would be stronger if the Cantici were left in suspense, others may be sensitive to the comic effect, others may point the moral.

Alternative approaches to this story can be found in *Independent Learning Manual* Stage 15 (suitable for students on a reduced timetable) and *Worksheet Master* 15.6.

Discussion

1 *Funeral games* were a respectful but cheerful event in memory of the dead (in this case the Emperor Claudius). This story is based on the funeral games for Anchises (Vergil's *Aeneid* V, 114–285). Cogidubnus' games have also a political function, to bring together the tribes he dominates, and demonstrate their allegiance to him and to Rome.

2 *The Celtic chieftains' behaviour.* Previous generations would have satisfied their touchy sense of personal honour in inter-tribal warfare.

Consolidation

1 It is unnecessary to re-read the whole of the story. Select a short passage, e.g. the first two paragraphs or the third paragraph, for the students to study in detail, possibly in pairs or groups, in order to produce a polished translation.

2 Ask students to look through the story again, collecting examples of superlative adjectives, or relative clauses, which you could use for oral revision.

3 Focus on words or phrases which revise a point of language or are important and hard to remember, and ask students to translate in context, e.g.:

Page 51
>   ibi (line 1), postrēmō (line 8).
>   aliae (line 3), cēterōs, alter (line 6).
>   aderant (line 2), praeerat (line 9).

Page 52
>   procul (line 1), mox (line 13), intereā (line 19), tum (line 22).
>   prior (line 3), fortiōrēs (line 12).
>   perīculōsum est … nāvigāre (lines 5–6), necesse est … vītāre (lines 6–7), facile est … vincere (line 11), difficile erat … vidēre (lines 22–3).

4 Ask students to record or write a sports commentary on the boat race.

About the language 2: imperfect tense of possum, etc. (p. 53)

New language feature. Imperfect tense of **possum**, **volō** and **nōlō**.

Discussion. Let the students use *was able* initially, to help them recognise the need for an infinitive to complete the sense of the verb, but they should become confident in using *could* by the end of paragraph 6. Compare the endings of **poteram** with those of **eram**.

Consolidation. List the personal endings -**m**, -**s**, -**t**, etc. vertically on the board. Point to an ending and ask the class to chorus the correct English pronoun. Proceed slowly at first, keeping to the regular sequence; then speed up, darting about. Repeat the exercise with endings listed in a scrambled order.

Practising the language (p. 54)

Exercise 1. Complete the sentences with a noun in the correct case, accusative or dative.
Exercise 2. Translation of short sentences containing an infinitive.

Language information: revision

Revision of the present tense of **sum**, **possum**, **volō** (p. 162) fits well with the consolidation work on the story **ad aulam** (p. 46) and with 'About the language 2' (p. 53).

Cultural background material (pp. 55–7)

Content. The contribution of Cogidubnus to the Roman invasion of Britain, and his position as a client king for the Romans. The evidence relating to Cogidubnus is best studied towards the end of the Stage, when students have met in the easier context of the stories some of the ideas that are discussed in greater depth here.

Discussion

- *Documentary evidence for Cogidubnus* exists in two places: the inscription on the temple to Neptune and Minerva (see illustration on p. 43, and drawing on p. 55); and a passage in Tacitus, *Agricola* 14: 'Certain territories were given to King Cogidubnus (he remained most loyal right down to our own times) according to an old and long accepted tradition of the Roman people, using even kings as instruments of slavery'.
- *The role of a 'client king'.* What help did Cogidubnus give the Romans, to earn this status? What were his responsibilities? How would this special relationship between Cogidubnus and the Romans be viewed by (a) the Romans, (b) his own subjects and (c) Cogidubnus himself?
- *The romanisation of Britain.* How was this achieved (*Worksheet Masters* 15.1 and 15.4)? What elements of Roman civilisation have survived to our own times?

Illustrations

p. 54 • Chichester from west (*Air photo Atmosphere*). Roman town walls at lower right. The two main streets intersect just beyond the cathedral. The one running up the centre veers north-east beyond the site of the east gate and becomes Stane Street, the road to London. Town walls, and streets intersecting at right angles, are characteristic of towns founded by the Romans.

p. 55 • Reconstruction of dedicatory inscription from the temple to
       Neptune and Minerva at Chichester, discovered in 1723. The text
       of the inscription is reproduced below.

       [ ] = missing part of stone; ( ) = expansion of abbreviation.
       [N]EPTVNO ET MINERVAE
           TEMPLVM
       [PR]O SALVTE DO[MVS] DIVINAE
       [EX] AVCTORITAT[E TI(BERI)] CLAVD(I)
       [CO]GIDVBNI R[EG(IS) MA]GNI BRIT(ANNORVM)
       [COLLE]GIVM FABROR(VM) ET QVI IN EO
       [SVN]T D(E) S(VO) D(EDERVNT) DONANTE AREAM
       ...]ENTE PVDENTINI FIL(IO)

p. 56 • Detail of mosaic (*Tunisia, Sousse Museum*). Neptune holding a
       fishing spear.
     • Discus of lamp (*Trier, Rheinisches Landesmuseum*). Minerva as
       Pallas Athena, wearing an aegis and carrying a spear and shield.
     • Model of two wooden granaries (*Fishbourne Museum*). Dated by
       coins and pottery to the early 40s AD, they probably relate to the
       invasion; possibly to the original military landings, more likely to
       the conquest of the south-west.

p. 57 • Colossal head of Vespasian (*Naples Archaeological Museum*).
     • Maiden Castle, near Dorchester, Dorset, from the west (*Air photo
       Francesca Radcliffe*). Note the area (19ha) and elaborate Iron Age
       gate defences, constructed 400–100 BC. Foundations of
       roundhouses, found during excavation, show this was a
       permanent settlement, an **oppidum**.
     • Durotrigan settlement at Hod Hill, Dorset (*Photo Francesca
       Radcliffe*). Good defensive position with land dropping steeply on
       three sides. Captured by Vespasian and modified as a Roman
       camp with two walls from the Iron Age structure. Roman
       gateways visible in other two walls.
     • Part of cemetery, eastern entrance to Maiden Castle, during
       excavation (*Photo copyright Society of Antiquaries*). Thirty-seven
       defenders, men and women, were buried by their people with
       food for their journey to the next world.

p. 58 • Detail of skeleton from Maiden Castle cemetery (*Photo Dorset
       County Museum, Dorchester*). The Romans fired volleys of artillery
       to cover the advance of the legionaries towards the gates, and this
       defender caught an arrow from a ballista in his spine.

Suggested activities

1 Draw up the entry on Cogidubnus for *Who's Who in Roman Britain*, as
  shown in *Independent Learning Manual* Stage 15.

2 Prepare a dialogue in pairs. Imagine you are:
  a an old Briton of the tribe of the Atrebates who knew Cogidubnus in his early days when he first welcomed the Romans,
  b the Briton's son, one of the young men whose journey to the palace was delayed by damage to the cart, giving his father his impressions of the events of the day.
3 In pairs, weigh up the information you have about Cogidubnus, and make three lists:
  a the facts you know for *certain*, and the evidence for them,
  b anything about him you think is *probably* true, with reasons for your opinion,
  c anything else you think could *possibly* be true, with reasons for your opinion.
  Find another pair who has carried out this task and compare your lists.
  Do they agree in every respect? If they do not, why do you think this is?

STAGE 16 in aulā

Cultural background	Story line	Main language features	Focus of exercises
The palace at Fishbourne.	Intent on revenge after his humiliation in the boat race, Belimicus plots to use a dancing bear to injure or kill Dumnorix. The plot misfires and the bear attacks the king, who is saved by Quintus' prompt action. Quintus tells the king about his travels since leaving Pompeii.	• Pluperfect tense. • Relative clauses introduced by **quōs, quās.**	Pluperfect tense and relative clauses.

Opening page (p. 59)

Illustration. Entrance to the audience chamber, in the centre of the west wing (see p. 69 for overview). Deliberately stage-managed to create maximum impact, it was approached from the gatehouse across the courtyard by a wide gravel path with hedges and lawns on either side. Built AD 75–80, when most Britons lived in roundhouses, it was very new at the time of the story, approximately AD 81 (*Model and photo Fishbourne Roman Palace*).

Model sentences (pp. 60–1)

New language feature. Pluperfect tense, and relative clauses introduced by **quōs** and **quās.**

New vocabulary. fōns, marmoreus, effundēbat, ōvum, saltātrīx, pilās, iactābant.

First reading. As the pluperfect tense is introduced within relative clauses, the sense usually guides students to the correct translation. Elicit *had* initially. If students say *pictures which a Greek artist painted*, ask 'Were they painted before Cogidubnus took Quintus round? Could you add a word before *painted* to make that clear?' In the same way passive renderings such as *painted by a Greek artist* should not be labelled wrong, but students should be guided to rephrase them. Do not comment on the accusative case of the relative pronoun unless the students question it. It is sufficient for them to grow accustomed to a variety of forms before discussion of the pronoun takes place.

    With sentences 1–3, refer students to the relevant picture essays on the palace (pp. 69, 70–1) and the palace gardens (pp. 72–3). Allow time for study and discussion of these photographs, so that the students develop a realistic context for the rest of the model sentences and the stories which follow.

Sentences 4–6 contain entertainments of a sort popular at extravagant Roman dinner parties (see Petronius, *Cena Trimalchionis*, Pliny, *Letters* 9, 17).

Consolidation. Throughout the Stage the reading passages will provide opportunities to ask the students to identify verbs in the pluperfect tense, comparing them with the model sentences, and translating them in context. Postpone any analytical discussion until 'About the language' (p. 66).

Belimicus ultor (p. 62)

Story. Belimicus, mortified by continuing ridicule, plans revenge on Dumnorix. He persuades the German slave in charge of the king's animals to let him handle the bear until he has tamed it, in readiness for a suitable opportunity.

First reading. Direct your comprehension questions towards the emotions of the characters, which are the motivation for the action in this story and its sequels, e.g.:

How did Belimicus react to his defeat in the boat race?
Which Latin words and phrases describe his mood?
What was the attitude of the guests towards Belimicus in his misfortune?
Did the Cantici feel the same as Belimicus about the defeat?
Is this true to life? Is this how losers behave?
What might Belimicus be thinking and feeling while he was training the bear?
What do you think Belimicus plans to do with the bear?
From what you know of Belimicus, do you think he will carry out his plan skilfully and successfully?

Consolidation. Oral practice of the present, perfect and imperfect tenses could be followed by the selection of a short passage containing a variety of tenses for written translation, e.g. **Belimicus, prīnceps ... cōnsilium callidum cēpit** (lines 1–9).

Illustrations
- Bronze statuette of dwarf holding castanets (*British Museum*).
- Detail from mosaic (*Trier, Rheinisches Landesmuseum*). The bear is leaning on a tree in the mosaic.
- Dancing girl from mosaic (*Trier, Rheinisches Landesmuseum*). What she holds in her hands is obscure. Encourage the students to speculate. Could they be flowers? Parts of a percussion instrument?

rēx spectāculum dat I (p. 63)

Story. Belimicus is jeered at by Dumnorix when he arrives late for the king's banquet. He watches the entertainment quietly until Salvius asks for the bear.

First reading. After the meaning is clear, probe deeper with questions, e.g.:
Why are Salvius and Quintus near the king?
Why do the Romans, not the Britons, show interest in wine?
What do you think of Dumnorix's taunts in lines 5–6?
Why does Belimicus make no reply to these taunts?
How do we know that the bear is well known before the story starts?
Which elements in Cogidubnus' hospitality were Roman? Why do you think he included them?
What do you think will happen if the bear is brought in?

Consolidation. Take the students through the vocabulary checklist (p. 74). Remind them of the format, discuss derivations and ask them to learn the vocabulary.

rēx spectāculum dat II (pp. 64–5)

Story. Belimicus challenges Dumnorix to handle the bear. Dumnorix boasts he can overpower the bear, and Belimicus too. In a fury, Belimicus pushes the bear at Dumnorix. Rounding on him, it lashes out. Panic ensues and, as the bear makes for the king's couch, Quintus seizes a spear and kills it.

First reading. Ask the class to follow the story as you read it through in Latin, and tell you of any sentences or phrases that they find difficult, so that you can work at these with them before they tackle the comprehension questions in pairs or individually. It is a good idea to read a third or a half of the story at a time in this way. The answers to the comprehension questions and the mark scheme are as follows. Give credit for any sensible answer.

		Marks
1	The German slave immediately came forward with the bear and showed it to the guests.	2
2	Belimicus boasted that he dared to handle the bear. He led the bear towards Dumnorix.	2
3	Belimicus challenged Dumnorix to handle the bear and to give a show to the guests.	2
4	Dumnorix said that it was easy for him to overpower the bear; he could also overpower Belimicus.	2
5	Belimicus struck the bear (in his rage) and pushed it towards Dumnorix.	2
6	The bear suddenly turned and ferociously struck Belimicus.	2

7 They made a great noise/shouted loudly; they rushed to the
   doors as quickly as possible.   2
8 The guests could not get out.   1
9 The noise had terrified the bear.   1
10 The king was lame.   1
11 a Dumnorix hurled himself at the bear in vain.   1
   b Salvius stood motionless.   1
   c Quintus seized the spear which the German slave was
     holding, quickly threw it and pierced the bear. *Give credit
     for any three sensible points.*   3
12 a Dumnorix was brave/but not very realistic.
   b Salvius was useless/was a coward/perhaps he did not
     want to help the king.
   c Quintus was resourceful/did not panic.   3
                                                         ──────
                                                   TOTAL 25

Discussion. After the end of this Stage, the main story line is interrupted
for four Stages while Quintus describes his travels. It is therefore
important at this point to make Cogidubnus' relationship with Salvius so
memorable that the students will return to it easily at the start of Book III.
Topics might include:

1 *Responsibility.* Who is really to blame for the accident? The German
  slave? Salvius for requesting that the bear be brought to the banquet?
  Belimicus? Dumnorix who provoked Belimicus to the point of
  desperation? Cogidubnus? Should he have foreseen trouble and put a
  stop to Dumnorix's provocation?
2 *Reputations.* What word might Salvius have used to describe the
  incident to Rufilla: accident, farce, riot? What impression do you think
  Salvius had of Quintus after the incident? Why did Salvius not
  intervene?

Consolidation. Language features which could be isolated for practice
include:

1 Relative clauses and their antecedents (see note on p. 50, above).
2 Tenses (present, imperfect, perfect) and the infinitive in preparation for
  the discussion of the pluperfect tense which follows in the next section.
  Oral practice could be followed by a written translation, e.g.: **rēx servīs
  … spectāculum dare vīs**?' (lines 1–12).

Illustration. Detail from the Great Hunt mosaic, Roman villa of early 4th
century AD, Piazza Armerina, Sicily (from *La Villa Erculia di Piazza
Armerina* by G.V. Gentili). Animal collectors are loading captured ostriches
onto a boat to be transported for the arena. The gang-plank can be seen at
the bottom. The capture of wild animals in the provinces was big business
and included: bears and wolves from Britain and Germany, lions from

north Africa, elephants from east and central Africa, crocodiles from the Nile. Most went to the arena but some wealthy Romans kept them in private zoos for show.

About the language: pluperfect tense (p. 66)

New language feature. Pluperfect tense.

Discussion. Take paragraphs 1–3 together. The pluperfect is introduced most naturally as the verb of the relative clause, but a causal clause is used in paragraph 3, example 5e. At this point, ask the students to look back to the model sentences and identify examples of the pluperfect tense and translate them. Then study paragraph 4. Elicit comments, e.g. 'The pluperfect starts like the perfect.'

Consolidation. Ask the students to find examples of the pluperfect tense in the previous story, and translate them in context. Turn to 'Language information' (p. 160) and compare the perfect and pluperfect tenses. Ask for the meanings of different persons, gradually increasing the speed of questioning. Put up on the board a list of jumbled perfect and pluperfect endings, **-erātis**, **-ērunt**, **-ī**, etc. and ask the class (with textbooks closed) to give the person and tense.

Quīntus dē sē (p. 67)

Story. Quintus tells the king how he escaped the eruption of Vesuvius, decided to travel abroad, and spent a few months in Athens before setting sail for Egypt.

First reading. This story should be treated as an introduction to the next Stage, and read at one sitting. Be prepared to help with:
> paterne et māter superfuērunt? (lines 3–4).
> ibi servum, quī tam fortis et tam fidēlis fuerat, līberāvī (lines 7–8).
> omnēs vīllās, quās pater in Campāniā possēderat, vēndidī (line 10).
> haec urbs erat pulcherrima, sed cīvēs turbulentī (line 15).

Sentences like the second and third examples above need considerable practice. See the further examples in the consolidation section on p. 39 of this Guide.

The following comprehension questions could be used:
> Where did the king have this conversation with Quintus?
> Why do you think the king was so friendly with Quintus?
> Who escaped with Quintus to Naples?
> How did Quintus raise money after the eruption of Vesuvius?
> Why did he want to leave Italy?
> Where did he go first? Whom did he see in the forum there?
> Where did he go next? How did he travel? Was the journey long or short?

Discussion questions should help students to recall characters and events, e.g.:

What were the names of Quintus' mother and father?

What is implied about the fate of Grumio and Melissa?

What is the name of Quintus' freedman?

Why is he described as **tam fortis et tam fidēlis**? (See Stage 12, **ad vīllam** and **fīnis**.)

Students could trace the journey of Quintus and Clemens on a map (*Independent Learning Manual* Stage 16 or *Worksheet Master* 16.1).

Consolidation. Use this passage to revise for the Attainment test to be completed at the end of this Stage. For example:

Ask the students to pick out all expressions of time and translate them in context. Practise short sentences with no stated nominative, and extend them, e.g.:

cēnam cōnsūmpsērunt.	cēnam, quam parāverāmus, cōnsūmpsērunt.
dominōs audīvimus.	dominōs, simulatque clāmāvērunt, audīvimus.
pecūniam invēnit.	pecūniam, quam āmīserās, invēnit.
mātrem vīdistis?	mātrem, postquam discessit, vīdistis?

Illustration. Acropolis, Athens, from south-west (*Photo John Deakin*). The upper buildings are 5th century BC: Propylaea, gateway to the Acropolis (left); Parthenon, temple of Athena (right). Below is the theatre of Herodes Atticus, 2nd century AD.

Practising the language (p. 68)

Exercise. Complete the verb in the relative clauses with the correct pluperfect ending. There are further exercises on the pluperfect and relative clauses in *Worksheet Masters* 16.2 and 16.5.

Language information: revision

Revise the pronouns **ego**, **tū**, **nōs**, **vōs** and **sē** (pp. 156–7).

Cultural background material (pp. 68–73)

Content. The palace of Fishbourne. The picture essays about the layout of the palace (p. 69), decor (pp. 70–1) and the gardens (pp. 72–3) provide a suitable introduction if taken with the model sentences. The complete account may be studied at any time during the Stage.

Discussion

1 What is the significance of the palace, in terms of the wealth it demonstrated, the Roman style and the location?

Wealth. Draw up a list of the different groups of craftsmen who worked on the palace, where they came from and the materials they used. Where would the money come from for such an elaborate house? Who would design it?

Style. Why should the occupant of the palace wish it to be built in Roman style? What would be its impact on the British chieftains? What would Quintus think of it? Do you think there were any disadvantages to living in a house like this in Britain?

Location. What were the reasons for the palace being built in this particular place?

2 Who is more important, Salvius or Cogidubnus? Encourage students to weigh up the evidence in the stories of Stages 13–16 of Cogidubnus' title and visible rank against Salvius' **rōmānitās** and links with the emperor.

Further information

The making of mosaics. The drawing of the making of a mosaic (below) is based on a black and white mosaic from Stabiae which was discovered in a half-laid state. A layer of mortar has a grid scratched into it, the design is outlined inside the grid in black paint (from the bowl at front), and is covered by the craftsman on the right with mortar from his trowel and chips of black or white stone from his box of prepared tesserae. The figure on the left is based on a relief from Ostia. It shows a craftsman chipping sawn sticks of rock into tesserae.

Illustrations

p. 68 ● Detail of model. The bath house can be recognised by its barrel vaulting (see Stage 9).

p. 69 ● Model of palace in its final form as seen from the south (cf. drawing, p. 47).

p. 70 ● Restored section of wall (top left). The red dado at base, and panels of plain colour framed with bright stripes, would contrast well with a black and white mosaic floor. The light blue panel shown here is surrounded by a frame of narrow lines in white, red, dark blue and yellow. The panels on either side are orange and the same darker blue as the frame.

- Fragment of landscape painting (top centre). There are thousands of fragments of painted plaster from Fishbourne, not all in plain colours. Some include candelabra, one shows a shrimp. This photo shows the corner of a picture in a yellow frame. The bottom half (not shown here) has part of a dark red-purple building, set against a blue-green background (top half), possibly water with flashes of light. The building consists of four white columns surmounted by a horizontal white architrave, with a triangular gable. Small impressionistic paintings like this are typical of the towns around Vesuvius.
- An example from Stabiae (top right), for comparison, shows a detail from the picture shown in full in Stage 3 (p. 27). Buildings rise up the hillside (right) overlooking the sparkling water of the harbour.
- Fragment of moulded stucco frieze (bottom left) from north wing. Two birds with fruit in their beaks stand on either side of vases of fruit topped with three apples. The frieze would have run round the top of the wall.
- A wall decoration, with original fragments of marble (bottom right).

p. 71
- Group of floors (top) from the time of Cogidubnus, worked entirely in black and white mosaic. Both upper examples are from one floor in the north wing of the palace using (right) curved motifs, composed from intersecting circles, to represent stylised flowers, and (left) straight lines to suggest cubes in three-dimensional perspective. Another floor from the north wing (centre left) shows a classic design of rectangles. A floor from the west wing (centre right) has the popular meander pattern also known as the Greek key pattern.
- Late 2nd century floor (below) from north wing, very large and elaborate. Central medallion has Cupid on dolphin, surrounded by four semi-circles with mythical sea creatures, sea horses and sea panthers (detail p. 74). Between the semi-circles are urns and corner designs of fluted shells. Typical Romano-British border with cable, curved triangles and scroll of stylised vegetation.

p. 72
- Garden replanted with clipped box hedges in alternate semi-circles and half-squares. Espalier fruit trees line the gravel path which crosses the picture at the top and continues down the right-hand side.
- Same stretch of garden during excavation, photographed from

opposite end, showing original bedding trenches cut in the gravel. The diagonal trenches are modern drains.

p. 73 • The garden flowers would have been grown for use as well as decoration. Acanthus (lining path below espalier fruit trees) was used to make a poultice for sprains, burns and hair loss. Lily oil was used in a cleansing face cream, and the juice was applied to ulcers and fresh wounds. Rose was popular for scenting the soles of the feet, and for eye infections which were prevalent among the Romans (see Stage 20). Hyssop attracted bees which provided honey, the only sweetening agent in the Roman world. Hyssop was made into perfumes and a linctus for coughs and chest problems including asthma.

• Reconstruction of potting shed, with slave putting compost into a pot. The pot on the bench, with drainage holes bored in sides and base, is a replica of one found during excavation. Once planted, it would be put in the earth, allowing the roots to feed from the soil around. Replica Roman tools on wall (left) are a sickle, and a pruning hook with curved point.

p. 74 • Sea panther, detail from mosaic on p. 71.

Suggested activities

1 Examine the mosaics on p. 71. Sketch the separate elements which are combined to make these patterns. Choosing from these, design on graph paper your own mosaic. For further patterns, see *Worksheet Master* 16.8.

2 Imagine you are Rufilla on a visit to London, and tell your neighbour about a visit you made to Cogidubnus' queen in her recently modernised palace. Remember to give details of the decoration and describe the garden.

3 Compose (and illustrate) an estate agent's advertisement for Fishbourne palace. *Worksheet Master* 16.7 has a pro forma.

4 If practicable, arrange a group visit to the palace (details from Curator, Fishbourne Roman Palace, Chichester, West Sussex PO19 3QR). It is possible to combine this with a visit to Butser, with its roundhouses and early Roman villa (details from Curator, Nexus House, Gravel Hill, Horndean, Waterlooville, Hampshire PO8 0QE).

5 Set Attainment test 1 (p. 83 of this Guide).

Vocabulary checklist

nōnne, like **num**, is treated as a vocabulary item only and no further explanations are given in the textbook. For teachers who wish to discuss **nōnne** and **num** in greater detail an exercise is provided in *Worksheet Master* 15.5.

STAGE 17 Alexandrīa

Cultural background	Story line	Main language features	Focus of exercises
Roman Alexandria: growth of the city, trade, key buildings, racial tensions.	Quintus describes what happened during his stay with Barbillus, a rich Alexandrian merchant, including a riot near the harbour and a visit to the temple of Serapis.	Genitive case.	1 Genitive case. 2 Imperfect and perfect tenses: 1st and 2nd person singular and plural. 3 Present tenses of **volō, possum.**

Opening page (p. 75)

Illustration. Alexandrian bronze coin, important evidence for the appearance of the Pharos, especially the proportions and the three tiers. From this and other coins, and written sources, it is clear that the tiers were square at the bottom, octagonal in the middle and circular at the top. Statues of four Tritons stood on the upper corners of the bottom tier, and Zeus the Saviour on the top. Note windows, and an entrance door at lower left.

Model sentences (pp. 76–7)

Story. Quintus describes to Cogidubnus his first impressions of Alexandria, and his arrival at the opulent house of Barbillus, a business connection of Caecilius.

New language feature. The genitive case is introduced in prepositional phrases.

New vocabulary. īnsula, pharus, prō templō, fūdī.

First reading. Introduce by oral recapitulation of **Quīntus dē sē** (p. 67), to reinforce the change of location which is illustrated in the line drawings. Elicit the fact that Quintus is accompanied by Clemens, his freedman. Students usually translate the genitives without difficulty because they are always preceded by sentences in which both nouns occur, e.g. **Alexandrīa magnum portum habet** leads naturally to **in portū Alexandrīae**. They use the translation *of* readily and, in sentences 4 and 5, some will suggest *Barbillus'*. Accept any correct translation, postponing discussion until 'About the language' (p. 80).

Be prepared to give help with the change to the 1st person plural in sentence 3, since the pronouns are omitted.

Consolidation. Use the drawings and sentences as a source of information, and then take the cultural background material (p. 84) at this point.
Possible questions:
Drawing 1. What features do you consider distinctively Egyptian?
Drawing 2. How many different kinds of people and activities can you see?
Drawing 3. Why are Quintus and Clemens unshaven? Why do you think Quintus is making an offering?
Drawing 4. What does the atrium suggest about Barbillus?

Illustrations

p. 76 • Pharos as described above, merchant ships, Cleopatra's Needles on the shoreline near the Caesareum (temple of the Imperial Cult), and temple of Serapis on the hill behind.

• Street scene including man with stubborn donkey, slaves engaged in maintenance work at the entrance to a temple, toga-clad Roman citizens, other men in tunics, a woman carrying an amphora, Roman military patrol, an argument in progress.

p. 77 • Quintus pours a libation on the altar. He and Clemens are unshaven, a sign of travel weariness.

• The atrium of a wealthy man, with elaborate mosaic and wall-paintings, impluvium and marble table, vista to study and garden with statues. The villa is in the Roman style, but shows an oriental preference for richly decorated surfaces.

tumultus I (p. 78)

Story. Quintus sets out to visit Clemens' shop near the harbour. Alarmed by the atmosphere in the streets, his slave-boy advises him to return, but he carries on.

First reading
in vīllā … maxima erat multitūdō (lines 1–10) presents a familiar street scene and, after your Latin reading, can be allocated to the students to translate in pairs. Help may be needed with the 1st person verbs. Remind students that Quintus is telling his story to Cogidubnus.
tandem ad portum … prōcēdere (line 10–end) builds suspense. Translate it with the class as a whole, in order to sustain momentum. Ask which word in the last line is the most significant, so that they notice how **cautē** heightens the suspense.

Consolidation. By listing ominous phrases on the board as they occur (**plūrimī Aegyptiī, nūllōs Graecōs, anxius, viae sunt perīculōsae, Aegyptiī īrātī, Graecī fūgērunt, cautē prōcēdere**), you can help the students to see how the writer builds up the tension. The list could be used again for vocabulary practice at the start of the next lesson.

tumultus II (pp. 78–9)

Story. Quintus and his slave come across an agitator haranguing the crowd of Egyptians and take refuge with a Greek craftsman. His house is attacked and in the riot the boy is killed.

First reading. Prepare the students for this comprehension passage by a lively Latin reading, and some preliminary translation of sentences which you consider may give them difficulty, e.g.: **puer Aegyptius … dūxit** (lines 5–6), **nam in casā … Graecōs vituperābant** (lines 14–15), **nōs Aegyptiīs … paucī** (lines 20–1). They might then attempt the questions individually or in pairs. The answers and mark scheme are as follows. Give credit for any sensible answer.

		Marks
1	The old man was cursing the Greeks and Romans. Everyone was listening to him intently.	2
2	Quintus was a Roman and was therefore worried by the old man's curses/the crowd were taking the curses seriously/he foresaw racial violence.	1
3	A craftsman, who knew Barbillus well, lived in the house. They would avoid danger inside *or similar.*	2
4	The craftsman happened to be looking through the window and recognised the boy.	2
5	Quintus was in the house of a Greek and the Egyptians were cursing the Greeks outside the door of the house.	2
6	Diogenes took out five clubs from a cupboard and gave them to us/Quintus and the boy.	2
7	The Egyptians broke down the door.	1
8	The Egyptians were many, we/those in the house were few.	2
9	Seven Egyptians surrounded Quintus; he seriously wounded two of them; the others overpowered him; he fell down unconscious. *Give three marks for any three good points.*	3
10	The boy.	1
	The Egyptians were afraid to kill a Greek or a Roman because they knew they would be punished, whereas they thought the death of a slave-boy was of no importance/they killed the Egyptian slave-boy, because he was defending a Roman.	2

TOTAL 20

Discussion

1 *The population of Alexandria.* Syrians, Jews and Egyptians competed vigorously with the Greeks for a share of trade, particularly in the mercantile area round the harbours. The Roman governor relied on military force to maintain public order (see line drawing 2 in model sentences, the last paragraph on p. 89 and p. 90).

2 *Motivation.* Why did Quintus ignore the slave-boy's advice? Who was responsible for the death of the slave-boy? Encourage the students to put forward a range of possible answers, supporting them with evidence from the text.

3 *Racial conflict.* Students might suggest modern parallels and discuss the characteristics, e.g.: hostility is easily aroused and erupts quickly into violence; it is directed at the nearest available target, and affects the innocent.

About the language: genitive case (p. 80)

New language feature. The genitive case is explained by means of examples already met in the stories.

Discussion will confirm observations made by the students, with your help, during the study of the model sentences. If students are unsure, ask them to translate one or two of the model sentences again. Encourage them to use the appropriate English for the context, in deciding between *of* and the apostrophe. This exercise will also revise students' knowledge of the use of the apostrophe in English.

In examining the forms of the genitive, take **cīvium** as it comes without entering into the rule about increasing genitive plurals.

Consolidation. After studying paragraphs 1 and 2, ask students to find and translate phrases incorporating the genitive in the stories on pp. 78–9, before tackling the new examples in paragraph 3. Further practice is provided in *Worksheet Masters* 17.1 and 17.2.

**ad templum (pp. 81–2)

Story. A bore called Plancus attaches himself to Quintus and Barbillus as they walk to the temple of Serapis. He pesters them with information about the city monuments until silenced by the start of the sacrifice.

First reading. Set the students to prepare in groups a translation suitable for acting to the class. This will take some time and provide an opportunity for you to visit the groups, helping with difficulties and ensuring that they have a correct version. After acting their scenes in English, some students may volunteer a performance in Latin.

Discussion will be a part of this process, focusing on what the students need in order to present the scene in a lively and realistic manner. Topics may include:

1 *Serapis* was the guardian deity of Alexandria, in conjunction with Isis (see note below on illustration on p. 82). His temple on the hilltop (see drawing 1, p. 76) overlooked the city. The altar was in front of the steps outside the temple where the people could watch the ceremony, and his

statue was kept in the inner sanctuary, visible only to the priests except when it was carried in festival processions.

2 *Barbillus' feelings.* Ask the students to find all the ways in which the writer shows what Barbillus is feeling.

Consolidation. Practise any features which were giving difficulty to the groups as you moved around. The story provides useful examples for revising the pluperfect tense and the relative clause (see 'Language information: revision', p. 48 of this Guide), and different forms of questions.

Illustrations

p. 81 from left to right:

- Mummy portrait of Artemidorus, AD 100–120, from Hawara (*British Museum*). He wears a white tunic and a wreath applied in gold leaf. Mummies in the Roman period often incorporated a wooden panel with a painted portrait of the dead person. This example combines a Roman style of painting and a Greek inscription with the Egyptian embalming ritual.
- Man of Roman appearance in his 50s or 60s, AD 100–120, from Hawara (*British Museum*).
- Sculptured head from Alexandria, 1st century BC (*British Museum*). Sensitively carved in hard green schist, it shows Greek idealism and the stylised simplicity characteristic of Egyptian work.

p. 82 from left to right:

- Basanite head of Serapis, 2nd century AD (*British Museum*). An amalgam of Zeus, Hades, Asclepius and Osiris, Serapis was created by the Greek rulers, the Ptolemies, to make Egyptian religion acceptable to the Greeks. He was worshipped with Isis as god of the dead, of healing and of corn. His popularity, like that of Isis (see Stage 19), became widespread. There was a temple of Serapis in York (the inscription from it is in the Yorkshire Museum), and a similar head to this one was found in the Walbrook, London. If the story **ad templum** is omitted, add the relevant information from the discussion section of the story.
- Mummy portrait, AD 140–160, from Hawara (*British Museum*). Probably a priest of Serapis because of the three locks of hair on his forehead, and the seven-pointed gold star on a silver band.
- Statue of sphinx with granite column 30m high, nicknamed Pompey's pillar. The latter was set up in AD 291 beside the temple of Serapis in honour of Diocletian, whose statue stood on top. It is the only monument from ancient Alexandria which has remained standing ever since.

Practising the language (p. 83)

Exercise 1. Complete the sentences with noun in genitive, singular or plural.

Exercise 2. Complete the sentences with perfect or imperfect tense, 1st and 2nd persons, singular or plural.

Exercise 3. Complete the sentences with the appropriate person of the present tense of **volō** or **possum**; a testing exercise because the pronouns are omitted, and the switch back to the present tense requires thought.

Language information: revision

Verb practice (pp. 160–1). Ask the students to cover up the tables of verbs and work through exercises 1 and 2 (if not previously done) and exercise 3 (p. 161). Refer to the tables only when the exercises are completed. Make up similar exercises, if required. Discuss the section 'Persons and endings' (p. 161) and do exercise 2, supplementing it with further examples if necessary. The *Independent Learning Manual* Stage 17 has additional exercises.

For consolidating relative clauses, see 'Pronouns III' (p. 159), but postpone discussion of gender until Stage 18.

Cultural background material (pp. 84–91)

Content. Alexandria, setting for the next four Stages, provides a contrast to Roman Britain. The magnificence of the city, its history and culture, its strategic position where east meets west and the trade routes cross, and its importance to the daily life of Rome itself, produced a ferment of nationalities and a wealth of opportunities.

Discussion

1 *The city of Alexandria.* Look at the photograph of the coin on p. 75. Why do you think the Alexandrians chose this image to represent their city? As the son of a banker and business man, what would Quintus most admire about Alexandria? What would he find striking about the buildings?

2 *Alexandria in the ancient world was unique* in size (population of about a million), cultural richness (a Greek city of learning in Egypt, now part of the Roman empire), economic importance (as a centre of trade, grain collection and glass production), and government (a traditional bureaucracy now under the emperor's personal control).

3 *Contrasts between life in Pompeii, Britain and Alexandria.* Levels of material comfort, cultural diversity, personal freedom, and the pace of life would vary sharply between these places, as well as between social groups.

Illustrations

pp. 84–5

- View of Alexandria, looking from the sea towards the lake. The Royal Quarter is on the Great Harbour, left of the causeway linking Pharos island to the mainland. A canal can be seen linking the Western Harbour, right of the causeway, to the Lake Harbour and the Canopic mouth (now silted up) of the Nile delta. The city walls, enclosing a grid-pattern of streets, start near the mouth of this canal. From the western gate nearby, the wide Canopus Street runs right across the city. The temple of Serapis in the south-western quarter of the city is slightly raised, and the temple of Isis Pharia is on the eastern end of Pharos island not far from the short causeway to the lighthouse (*Painting Jean-Claude Golvin*).

p. 86
- Posthumous head of Alexander the Great, from Alexandria (*British Museum*). Alexander was said by the Romans to be one of the first people to manage his public image. He wanted to emphasise his youthfulness at the time of his conquests (he died at age 32) and selected artists capable of conveying this likeness, which became associated with him as a divinity after his death. This statue shows the attributes described in the literary sources: upward glance, leonine mane of hair, melting look in the eyes.
- For coin, see note on p. 43 of this Guide.
- Modern harbour at Alexandria (*Photo George Hart*).

p. 87
- Map of Roman empire, end of 1st century AD, showing principal trade routes and strategic position of Alexandria.

p. 88
- Reconstruction of the Pharos with cutaway showing the spiral ramp used by animals to carry fuel for the fire kept permanently alight at the top. Colossal statues of King Ptolemy and his queen can just be seen to the left of the tower (*Painting Jean-Claude Golvin*).
- Site of Pharos, with 15th century Fort Qaitbay (*Photo Stéphane Compoint/Sygma*).

p. 89
- Left: Cleopatra's Needles, 18th century print from *Description de l'Egypte* by Cecile, 1798 (*British Museum*). The obelisks were erected in Heliopolis by Thotmes III in 1475 BC and moved to the Caesareum in Alexandria by Augustus. The erect obelisk is now in New York, the other in London.
- Right: Cleopatra's Needle, obelisk approx. 21m high, on Thames Embankment.

p. 90
- Head of Medusa from an opulent house in Alexandria, first half of 2nd century AD. The room is a dining-room because this design is intended to face the doorway; the remaining three sides have a plainer design, which would have been covered by the dining-

couches. The central medallion, in very small tesserae, was prepared on a terracotta tray and inserted complete.

p. 91 • The marine archaeological project illustrated in the next three pictures was prompted by modern harbour works in 1984 and still continues.

p. 92 • Warships passing in a harbour. Unlike transport vessels, they were powered by rowers for flexibility, speed and accuracy. That on the left, moving towards the observer, has a battering ram on the front at the level of the water; that on the right has two steering oars projecting on either side of the stern.

Suggested activities

1 Imagine you are the Roman governor of Alexandria, personally accountable to the emperor. Write to the emperor explaining the causes of the riot, and reporting on the steps you are taking to prevent a recurrence.

2 You have now seen something of Roman life in Pompeii, Britain and Alexandria. Where would you rather have lived and why?

3 A good exercise on Alexandrian trade in *Independent Learning Manual Stage 17* can be used in conjunction with the map on p. 87.

4 *Worksheet Master* 17.7 has an exercise on the Seven Wonders of the Ancient World.

STAGE 18 Eutychus et Clēmēns

Cultural background	Story line	Main language features	Focus of exercises
Glassmaking in Alexandria; government and economy of Egypt, peasant farmers.	Clemens, new owner of a glass shop previously wrecked by thugs, visits the ring-leader and refuses to pay him protection money. His shop is attacked and he confronts the thugs, who are scared away by the sacred cat of Isis.	Gender; agreement of adjectives and relative pronouns in gender.	1 Agreement of adjectives. 2 Nominative singular and plural. 3 Pluperfect singular and plural. Relative pronouns and antecedents.

Opening page (p. 93)

Illustration

Fragments of shattered glass symbolise the violence that wrecked Clemens' glass shop and characterised the protection racket described in this Stage. Two glassmaking techniques are illustrated:

1 Wheel-cut glass (*largest fragment*), the technique used in modern cut crystal, was highly skilled and expensive. Outer side of transparent beaker showing huntsman, spear at the ready, wearing a billowing cloak, with part of hunting dog visible to right. Third century BC (*Murano, Museo Vetrario*).

2 Mould-blown glass (*next largest*) is much less expensive. Fragment of transparent beaker, decorated with scenes of chariot racing (*Murano, Museo Vetrario*).

Broken glass (called cullet) is an important ingredient in glassmaking. The background sherds here are modern, but Roman cullet has been found.

taberna (pp. 94–5)

Story. Quintus wants to buy a shop for Clemens. Hesitantly Barbillus offers him a shop, which had been vandalised and its owner killed by a gang operating a protection racket. Confident of Clemens' toughness and luck, Quintus buys it.

First reading. Read one paragraph at a time in Latin, and ask the students to translate, using a different method each time, e.g. oral, written, individual response, work in groups.

Discussion

1 *Clemens' character*. Quintus says Clemens is brave and lucky. Do the students agree? Refer back to Stage 12 if necessary.
2 *Word order*. The writer uses the final position in the sentence to good effect in this story. **dubitābat** (line 6) signals a surprising switch of mood, **mortuum** (line 10) adds dramatic impact, **trādidī** (line 17) introduces suspense as Quintus seals a contract with unforeseen consequences.

Consolidation. Concentrate on cases, selecting short phrases and asking students to identify the cases of the nouns, or noun and adjective pairs, in context. The first paragraph, which contains recent language features, is useful as a test translation.

Illustrations
p. 94 • Eutychus (left), with his thugs, is confronted by Clemens in a bar.
p. 95 • Thugs kill the old man who has refused to pay protection money.

in officīnā Eutychī I (p. 96)

Story. When Clemens visits his new shop, he finds it vandalised, and is told to question Eutychus, who is in the biggest workshop, guarded by four huge slaves. Refusing to be overawed, Clemens walks in past the astonished slaves.

First reading. As you read the story aloud in Latin, emphasise the threatening atmosphere. The students' understanding of the narrative can be checked by simple comprehension questions, and their appreciation heightened by more detailed discussion, e.g.:

1 **in viā vitreāriōrum** (line 4). What are the advantages and disadvantages of having all the glass shops in one street?
2 Why was the crowd **ingēns** in this street? Worshipping Isis? Shopping? Looking at the vandalised shop?
3 What was Clemens' reaction to the sight of his shop? How different was it from the reaction of the neighbouring shopkeeper?
4 Why does Clemens call the slave Atlas? Look at the illustration on p. 122.
5 Why does Clemens refer to himself as **lībertō** rather than **mihi** (line 17)?

valvās ēvulsās vīdit, tabernam dīreptam (lines 5–6). Accept the simple translation *He saw the wrenched off doors, the ransacked shop*, but encourage better alternatives such as *He saw the doors (were) wrenched off and the shop ransacked*.

officīnam Eutychī (line 18). A genitive depending on a nominative or an accusative noun will be extensively practised in Stage 19. This occurrence causes no difficulty and needs no comment.

Consolidation. Now that Clemens is a freedman, he can act on his own initiative. Twice in this story he acts **statim** (lines 2 and 10). Ask the students to go through the story again in groups, making a collection of the phrases or incidents which tell them something about his character. They could then share their findings with the rest of the class.

in officīnā Eutychī II (pp. 96–7)

Story. Clemens is greeted contemptuously by Eutychus, until he reveals his identity. Then he is treated to a tour of the impressive glassworks and offered protection, at a price. Clemens refuses and leaves.

First reading. Read each of the following scenes of the story in Latin, then translate and discuss.

Eutychus in lectō ... nunc mea est (lines 1–7) indicates the character of Eutychus as revealed by his personal habits and conversational style.

Eutychus, postquam ... vibrābat (lines 8–11). The tour of the workshops can be taken with the background information (pp. 105–7) to build up a picture of the glassmaking industry which Clemens has joined.

Eutychus, postquam ... exiit (line 12–end). The confrontation between Clemens and Eutychus offers an opportunity to discuss protection rackets, e.g.:
1 What would Clemens be buying for his ten gold pieces?
2 How does that compare with the price of the shop?
3 Would you pay it?

Consolidation. This passage is useful for class dramatisation. Young students may enjoy miming the glassmaking activities. There are exercises on glassmaking in *Independent Learning Manual* Stage 18, and *Worksheet Master* 18.7.

Illustrations
- Base from Portland vase (so-called because it was owned by the 3rd Duke of Portland), probably 1st century AD (*British Museum*). The vase had its original base replaced in ancient times with this disc, probably cut from a larger plaque. It shows Paris in his Phrygian cap holding a thoughtful finger to his lips as he judges the charms of Juno, Minerva and Venus. The cameo technique involves carving into the top layer to show a different-colour glass behind.
- Painted glass goblet, Egyptian, 1st century AD (*Paris, Musée Guimet*). This is one of a collection of 25 goblets found in Afghanistan, just inside the empire of Alexander the Great. It shows Europa and the bull, with Cupid to left. Below, a frieze of shields, showing a yellow shield lying over a blue one.

Clēmēns tabernārius (pp. 98–9)

Story. Clemens gains the trust of his neighbours, including the priests of Isis and the temple cat. When the shopkeepers refuse to pay up, Eutychus blames Clemens and arms his thugs.

First reading. Read the story aloud in Latin and give the students time to study it and seek help with problems before they attempt the comprehension questions, so that they gain success and develop confidence from the exercise. The answers and mark scheme are as follows. Give credit for any sensible answer.

		Marks
1	He hired craftsmen who repaired the doors and walls.	2
2	Clemens was friendly; he would often help them.	2
3	Near the temple of Isis. Clemens used to go to the temple every day.	2
4	He used to worship the goddess and would often dedicate a glass ornament to her.	2
5	They gave him a sacred book in which he could read about the secret worship of the goddess.	2
6	In the sanctuary of the temple.	1
	Clemens always stroked the cat and gave it something from his plate.	2
7	The shopkeepers/**tabernāriī**.	1
8	**inimīcum**. They refused to hand over money to him.	2
9	Clemens was a great nuisance; he must be punished.	2
10	Beat up Clemens and vandalise his shop.	2
	TOTAL	20

Consolidation. Ask students to find the four infinitives in the story (lines 10, 11, 17, 21) and give their meanings. If they need to revise infinitives, refer them to 'Language information', p. 160.

Illustrations

p. 98 • Clemens in his shop. Ask 'Why do you think the cat is there?' The Egyptians kept cats as pets, and as hunters to protect the granaries, and they venerated them as sacred animals. See the illustrations and text on p. 103.

p. 99 • Marbled glass (left) had colours mixed together to suggest agate, or other semi-precious stones. Glassmaking probably started in imitation of vessels carved from rock crystal and other ornamental stones.

• Small flask (right) is probably mould-blown.

About the language: gender (pp. 100–1)

New language feature. Gender is introduced in the context of adjectives agreeing with nouns.

Discussion. Work through paragraphs 1–4 with the class. Then look at the first page of the Vocabulary (p. 170), showing how 1st and 2nd declension adjectives are listed with the forms for masculine, feminine and neuter. Reinforce this by asking them which form of **avārus** (*mean*) they would use to describe a woman, and which form of **antīquus** (*ancient*) to describe a temple, etc. Further written examples should be set in a familiar context, e.g.:

1 Clēmēns Quīntō grātiās maximās ēgit.
2 in viā vitreāriōrum erat ingēns turba.
3 Clēmēns tabernārium vicīnum rogāvit, 'quis hoc fēcit?'
4 Eutychus officīnam maximam habēbat.
5 Clēmēns servōs attonitōs praeteriit.
6 omnēs tabernāriī Eutychō pecūniam dedērunt.
7 'praesidium tuum recūsō', inquit Clēmēns.
8 lībertus fortis exiit.

Consolidation. Take a story which the students have read, and ask questions which they answer with the text open, gradually introducing variations if appropriate. For instance, on p. 98:

1 **quī valvās refēcērunt** (lines 1–2). Whom does this relative clause describe? What is the gender of **fabrōs**? And of **quī**?
2 Look up the gender of **ōrnāmentum vitreum** (line 7), **librum sacrum** (line 10), **fēlēs sacra** (line 12).
3 Which word does **plūrimōs** (line 14) describe? What is the gender?
4 What case is **plūrimōs amīcōs**? What would be the meaning of **plūrimī amīcī** if the sentence read **plūrimī amīcī Clēmentem adiuvābant**?

There are further exercises in *Independent Learning Manual* Stage 18, and *Worksheet Masters* 18.1, 18.2, 18.3 and 18.6.

Illustration. Decorative panel from a wall (see note below for the illustration on p. 110).

prō tabernā Clēmentis (pp. 102–3)

Story. As his shop is attacked, Clemens confronts Eutychus and his thugs. They dare not touch him with the temple cat perched on his shoulder, and run away when it assaults Eutychus.

First reading. Take briskly to maintain the momentum of the story to its climax. Read the story aloud in Latin, to help the students recognise subordinate clauses. The long sentence **quondam, ubi ... cōnspexit accurrentem** (lines 2–3) contains two subordinate clauses, one 'nesting' inside the other. The commas (as well as your Latin reading) will help the students to recognise the boundaries of the clauses.

Discussion
1 What advice did his friend give Clemens in line 6? What were the reasons for giving this advice (lines 7–8)?
2 What does the word **immōtus** (line 10) tell you about Clemens' state of mind?
3 What is the meaning of **mī dulcissime!** (line 14)? Was Eutychus sincere?
4 Why did Clemens reply **cum summā tranquillitāte** (line 17)?
5 Why was Eutychus **īrātissimus** (line 20)?
6 **Clēmēns cōnstitit** (lines 23–4). How do you explain Clemens' confidence? Was it due to his new status as a freedman, or his religious faith (for more on Egyptian religion, see next Stage), or had life as a slave taught him to stand up for himself?
7 Why was Clemens alone?
8 **Eutychus ... perterritus fūgit** (line 35). Do you find the behaviour of Eutychus and his thugs credible?

Consolidation. Refer to 'Longer sentences I' (p. 167) to revise subordinate clauses introduced by **postquam**, **quod**, **quamquam** and **simulac**.

Illustrations
• The 'Gayer-Anderson' cat, c. 600 BC (*British Museum*), named after the man who presented it to the Museum. The anatomy is remarkably accurate. Made of bronze inlaid with silver, it wears gold rings at ears and nose, and a silver amulet of the eye of Horus around its neck.
• Spell 17 from a papyrus *Book of the Dead*, 1280 BC (*British Museum*). These books were collections of spells, commonly buried with the dead to help them in the next world. The cat was described in one tomb as a form of the sun-god Ra, who vanquishes darkness daily and brings prosperity. The cat in the illustration is based on the wild cat, *felis serval*.

Practising the language (p. 104)

Exercise 1. Complete the sentences by selecting an adjective to agree with the noun.
**Exercise 2.* Complete the complex sentences by selecting a noun or phrase to agree with the main verb.
Exercise 3. Complete the sentences by selecting the correct verb for the relative clause. Identify the noun described by the relative clause, and give the gender of the noun and the relative pronoun. Students may have to look up the gender of some nouns.

Language information: revision

Revise irregular verbs (pp. 162–3), giving special attention to the forms of

ferō, and translate the examples in paragraph 3. Make up further oral and written exercises, if necessary.

Word order has become more varied in this and the previous Stage (see the language synopsis on p. 81 of this Guide). If students are having problems with particular word orders, use appropriate examples from p. 165.

A second look at infinitives (p. 160), and 'Longer sentences I' (p. 167), has already been indicated.

Cultural background material (pp. 105–9)

Content. The section on glassmaking in Alexandria is best taken with **in officīnā Eutychī** (p. 96). The section on Egypt deals with the ruthless control exercised by the bureaucracy over the peasants, the corruption that resulted, and the exploitation of agricultural and manufacturing production for the benefit of the country's rulers. The unchanging nature of the life of the Egyptian people down the centuries, whoever was ruling them, means that illustrative material gathered from different periods is relevant to these stories set in the 1st century AD.

Discussion

1 *Modern parallels.* Ask students if they know of protection rackets or instances of bribery in public or private life.
2 *Social unrest in the empire.* Other examples can be found in the New Testament, e.g.: the riot of the silversmiths (Acts 19 vv. 23–41), and the Jewish riot against Paul (Acts 21 vv. 27 ff.), which is interesting because of the reactions of the Roman commander.

Illustrations

p. 105 • Scent bottle, 2nd–1st century BC (*British Museum*). The sand core, bound with clay, was held on the end of a rod which the craftsman revolved, trailing glass onto it in viscous strands of different colours. While still moist, the strands were combed upwards to produce the scalloped pattern, and the surface was smoothed (marvered) by rolling on a smooth surface. Handles were added separately.

  • Ribbon-glass bowl, 8.7cm high, 1st century BC – 1st century AD (*USA, Corning Museum of Glass*).

p. 106 • *Millefiori* bowl, 1st century BC – 1st century AD (*USA, Corning Museum of Glass*).

  • Line drawing of ancient glassworks. The crucible for molten glass is heated with the aid of bellows. The near craftsman is seated on a chair with a special ledge for rolling the blowing iron repeatedly to prevent the 'gather' of glass at its end from flopping out of shape while he works on it. Note the variety of tools, metal and wood, for shaping and measuring the glass to conform with the designs drawn on the wall behind him.

- *Cumbria Crystal Glassworks, Ulverston, Cumbria.* The modern craftsman is inflating a 'gather' of molten glass which he has picked up by dipping his blowing iron into a crucible of molten glass inside the furnace. When he has blown the glass into a bubble he will work on a seat with a ledge, rolling his blowing iron repeatedly, and shape the glass with tools similar to those of the ancient glassworker.

p. 107
- Glass bird, 1st century AD, 11.7cm long with restored tail (*USA, Corning Museum of Glass*). The bird was possibly a container for perfume or face powder (traces found), and the user had to break the end off the tail to reach the contents. It is an example of the subtlety of form obtainable by simple manipulation of the bubble on the end of a blowing iron. To complete it, the craftsman transfers it from the blowing iron to a metal rod (punty), attached underneath the bird, so that the beak and tail can be drawn out with tongs (see left-hand side of line drawing on p. 106).
- Blown jug, opaque white, 15.2cm (*British Museum*).
- Mould-blown scent bottles were made in a variety of shapes, e.g. date, shell, bird, human head.

p. 108
- For much of the length of the Nile, the land made fertile by annual inundations was a narrow strip, menaced by the desert behind.
- Peasants harvesting corn, painted relief, 3rd millennium BC, tomb at Saqqara.
- Unpainted relief, 3rd millennium BC, tomb of Mereruke, high-ranking official. Two scribes checking estate accounts write on papyrus.

p. 109
- Charta Borgiana, AD 192–3 (*Naples Archaeological Museum, Egyptian Gallery*).
- Painted relief from temple of Rameses II (1279–1213 BC), Abydos. The Nile deity carries on a tray the fruits of the earth, birds and lotus flowers. Hanging from his arm are two ankhs, symbols of life (see illustration, p. 111). Since the building of the Aswan High Dam, the Nile no longer floods every year.

p. 110
- Decorative wall panel (see also pp. 100–1), Egyptian in style, mosaic of shaped pieces of glass and stone (opus sectile), Basilica of Junius Bassus, Rome, 4th century AD (*Rome, Museo Nazionale Romano*). It illustrates the enduring fascination Egypt held for the Romans.

Suggested activities

1 Written assignments:
   You are the Greek whose payments are listed on p. 109. Using the information given, make up a story to explain one or more of your bribes.
   Quintus says of Clemens (p. 95) 'vir fortis est. fortūna semper eī favet'. After reading the whole Stage, do you agree with Quintus? Do you consider good fortune or bravery more important?

2 Research assignment:
   Study the illustrations of different glassmaking techniques, and find modern examples, e.g.: bottles made in moulds (you can see where the two halves of the mould join to each other and to the base), *millefiori* in paperweights, cut glass in tumblers, jugs, bowls, etc. Draw and label them.

3 If possible, arrange to visit a glassworks in operation, or a good gallery. The new Glass Gallery in the Victoria and Albert Museum has examples from all periods, with explanation of their manufacture. The British Museum has many examples of ancient glass.

4 Set Attainment test 2 (pp. 83–5 of this Guide).

STAGE 19 Īsis

Cultural background	Story line	Main language features	Focus of exercises
The worship of Isis: spring festival, initiation, spread of worship.	Aristo, a friend of Barbillus, takes Quintus to the spring festival in honour of Isis. Barbillus invites them on a crocodile hunt.	• hic and ille. • Imperative; nōlī, nōlīte. • Vocative.	1 hic and ille. 2 Recognition of cases.

Opening page (p. 111)

Illustration. Detail from the papyrus of Queen Nedjmet, *c.* 1050 BC (*British Museum*). This shows the Egyptian representation of Isis, holding a sceptre in her right hand, and an ankh (symbol of life) in her left. Above her head is the hieroglyph of a throne, which is her name in hieroglyphs. After studying the picture, read pp. 126–7 which give more information about Isis and provide a context for the model sentences.

Model sentences (pp. 112–13)

Story. The family of Aristo, a friend of Barbillus, watches the procession of Isis.

New vocabulary. corōnās rosārum.

New language feature. hic: nominative and accusative singular in all genders, nominative and accusative plural in masculine and feminine.

The use of the genitive, first introduced in prepositional phrases in Stage 17, is extended here to include phrases where it is dependent upon a noun in the nominative or accusative. The students grasp this without the need for explanation.

Consolidation. Oral practice with phrases or sentences met here helps to establish the new characters and context, and forms a useful introduction to subsequent stories, especially **Aristō** (p. 114).

Aristō (p. 114)

Story. Aristo's unhappiness is explained. His wife entertains noisy musicians and his daughter attracts disruptive satirical poets, both inimical to the quiet reflections of a tragic poet. The students will no doubt supply modern parallels.

First reading. Introduce each paragraph with oral practice of the relevant model sentence on p. 112, and read it aloud in Latin, asking comprehension questions to help the students to understand the family and its conflicts over popular culture and serious art.

Consolidation. Ask the students to identify and translate phrases incorporating the genitive. Invite them to write a diary entry in English for Galatea, Helena or Aristo, based on this story and describing their lives and different points of view.

Illustrations

- The Roman theatre at Alexandria, looking from behind the stage towards the auditorium which seated 800 spectators.
- Mosaic of playwright, late 2nd to early 3rd century AD (*Tunis, Bardo Museum*). The poet is perhaps the comic dramatist Menander, planning his play by reflecting on the masks of comic characters. (Only one mask is visible here.)

diēs fēstus I (p. 115)

Story. Barbillus, unwilling to attend the spring festival, arranges for Quintus to go with Aristo and his family. As they approach the harbour, Galatea nags continually.

First reading. Help the students to recognise the joyful and expectant mood of the first paragraph by your Latin reading, and by drawing their attention to the language, e.g.: the lively effect of the two short sentences at the beginning, the heightened anticipation of the repeated **iam** (lines 1–2), the reference to the goddess as a person rather than a statue (line 2), and the excitement of the annual festival **sacerdōtēs ... erat** (lines 2–4).

Trust the students to read the rest of the story on their own or in pairs, only offering help if necessary, e.g. with the word order of **viās ... Alexandrīnī** (lines 10–11). If you keep a list of items the students find hard, you can practise them orally at the beginning or end of subsequent lessons.

Consolidation. Ask the students to translate the sentence **ego ... numquam** (lines 6–7), emphasising the contrast. Then ask them to translate other sentences with this shape which they have already met, e.g.:

> sed illī erant multī, nōs paucī (p. 79, line 21).
> tabernāriī mihi pecūniam dant, ego eīs praesidium (p. 96, Part II, lines 16–17).
> tabernāriī Eutychum inimīcum putābant, Clēmentem vindicem (p. 98, lines 16–17).

They could then translate others where the effect is not contrast, but emphasis, e.g.:

> fenestrae erant frāctae, casa dīrepta (p. 79, lines 24–5).
> valvās ēvulsās vīdit, tabernam dīreptam (p. 96, Part I, lines 5–6).
> multī fūrēs ad hanc viam veniunt, multī latrōnēs (p. 96, Part II, lines 14–15).

Illustration. Egyptian mummy portrait (*Stuttgart, Württembergisches Landesmuseum*), dated around AD 100, painted in encaustic (pigment mixed with heated wax) on a panel, which was then cut down and glued into the mummy wrappings with bitumen, of which traces can be seen in the black splodges at bottom right and left. The inscription across the neck, *Eirene, daughter of S... May her soul rise before Osiris, the great god, for ever,* is interesting for the Greek name combined with the Egyptian burial rite. She wears a green tunic, with a red mantle over her shoulder, a gold wreath of myrtle leaves and berries, and pearl earrings.

diēs fēstus II (pp. 116–17)

Story. Finding Aristo had forgotten to send a slave to keep good places for them at the temple of Augustus, Galatea dislodges two young men.

First reading. Encourage the students to prepare for the comprehension exercise by reading through the story in pairs, seeking your help as necessary. The answers and mark scheme are as follows. Give credit for any sensible answer.

		Marks
1	The name of the temple was the Caesareum/begun by Cleopatra as a shrine to Marcus Antonius/completed by Augustus as a temple to himself. *Also accept that Quintus poured a libation in front of the temple on his arrival.*	1
2	They were used to seeing the whole show from there.	1
3	The slave kept the place for them.	1
4	Aristo realised that he had forgotten to send the slave out in the morning *or similar*.	2
5	She saw two young men occupying her chosen place.	1
6	She told him to move the young men out of the way. She suspected that he hadn't sent the slave out (to keep the place).	2
7	Aristo suggested that it would be better to look for a new place. He said that the slave had obviously been negligent.	2
8	He asked for the place politely.	1
9	She shouted violently. She told the young men to give way and not obstruct them.	1 2
10	They were scared of Galatea and were smitten with Helena (and obviously did not want to ruin their chances).	2
11	The procession arrived/the crowd at once started shouting/ Galatea had got her own way.	1
12	Aristo was absent-minded because he forgot to send out the slave/nervous about being asked to move the young men/ a coward because he shifted the blame onto the slave/ conciliatory in the way he approached the young men/	

dominated by Galatea because he allowed her to take charge
of the whole situation.

3

TOTAL 20

Consolidation. A good story for dramatisation (starting from p. 115, line 13). Ask the students to make a collection of all the Latin verbs for speaking used in Parts I and II of the story, e.g. **inquit**, **vituperābat**.

Illustrations. This series of mummy paintings is remarkable for the youth of the subjects. It is possible that the paintings were prepared in life. However, census returns from Roman Egypt confirm the low life expectancy at the time. A number of mummies, like the young boy (last male figure to right), have been subjected to Computerised Axial Tomography (CAT) scans which reveal the correspondence of age between the body and the painting. From left to right:

- Man, encaustic on limewood, AD 80–100, from Hawara (*British Museum*), wearing white tunic with purple stripe, typical of men in mummy portraits, and white mantle.
- Young woman, encaustic on wood, AD 130–150, from Antinoopolis (*Louvre*), wearing dark blue tunic over white under-tunic with little purple triangles along the neckline, and gold earrings in the shape of bunches of grapes.
- Curly-headed man, encaustic on wood, mid-3rd century AD, unknown provenance (*Louvre*), wearing white tunic with two small dark decorations at the neck, and dark red mantle.
- Girl, encaustic on wood, AD 117–138, from Antinoopolis (*Louvre*). The neck, shoulders and pendant were initially painted, and afterwards covered in gold leaf. Her earrings have two pearls separated by a coloured stone. Her hair is drawn back into a coiled bun and fixed in place with a gold pin.
- Woman, encaustic on limewood, AD 110–120, from Hawara (*British Museum*), wearing cyclamen-mauve tunic and mantle, gold hoop earrings set with three round emeralds, and two necklaces. The upper is of emeralds and gold, the lower of amethysts with a large central emerald from which hang two pearls.
- Man of Greek appearance, encaustic on wood, AD 130–161, provenance unknown (*Moscow, Pushkin Museum*), wearing white tunic and mantle.
- Young boy, encaustic on wood, AD 100–120, from Hawara (*British Museum*), wearing white tunic and mantle. The portrait is still framed in the mummy wrappings.
- Woman, tempera (water-based paint) and encaustic on limewood, AD 60–70, from er-Rubayat (*London, National Gallery*), wearing crimson tunic with a black stripe edged with gold, darker crimson mantle, gold ball earrings, and plaited gold chain round her neck above a gold and emerald necklace.

About the language 1: hic and ille (p. 118)

New language feature. The nominative and accusative cases of **hic** and **ille**.

Discussion. If students ask about a neuter plural form, confirm that it exists but has not yet occurred in the stories.

Consolidation. For further practice on **hic**, return to the model sentences (pp. 112–13) and ask the students to identify the case, number and gender of each example of **hic** and its accompanying noun. **diēs fēstus II** (p. 116) can be used in the same way to practise **ille**. Alternatively, make up English sentences, e.g. 'I saw this girl', and ask what the Latin would be for 'this' in the context of the sentence. Additional exercises can be found in *Independent Learning Manual* Stage 19, and *Worksheet Master* 19.3.

**pompa (pp. 119–20)

Story. As the procession passes, Helena and Galatea make remarks about what they see, and the young men make remarks about them, eventually barging into Galatea. She criticises Helena for siding with them and Aristo for his lack of care.

First reading. This story may be taken as an amusing incident, or as a study of the family's characters, or as an illustration of the general point that people tend to notice what interests them. Read it straight through without comment, and then ask questions to encourage discussion.

Discussion

1 *Behaviour and character.* What do you think of Galatea's behaviour to the young men? Is she fair to Aristo? Describe the difference in the way Aristo behaves to other people. Why is he an unhappy man?

2 *What people notice.* What features of the procession does Helena notice and comment on? What catches Galatea's eye? Do the young men mind not having a good view of the procession? What do they comment on?

3 *The point of the story.* Which do you learn more about: the procession or the spectators? Do you find the story amusing? Give a reason.

Consolidation. Ask the students to draw a sketch or diagram of the procession, based on the model sentences (p. 113), this story, and the cultural background material (p. 126). An alternative exercise is *Worksheet Master* 19.2.

Illustrations

p. 119 • The image of Isis shows her in her likeness of the mother goddess Hathor, whose symbol is the disc of the sun encircled by horns (Hathor is often shown as a cow).

p. 120 • Tragic mask in marble from Villa of Tiberius, Sperlonga, Italy.

This is a good point at which to complete the reading of the background material on pp. 128–9.

About the language 2: imperatives (p. 121)

New language feature. Imperative singular and plural, including **nōlī, nōlīte**.

Discussion. Make sure that students understand the reason for the infinitive in negative commands.

Consolidation. After studying the note, ask the class to collect all the instructions issued by the bossy Galatea in recent stories. You could give some orders yourself and invite volunteers to carry them out, e.g.: **exī! venī hūc! sedē! dormīte! nōlīte dormīre! scrībite!** Then ask two or three students to give orders to the teacher and the class. Further practice is provided in *Worksheet Master* 19.5 and *Independent Learning Manual* Stage 19.

vēnātiō I (p. 122)

Story. Barbillus, leaving for a day's hunting with Quintus and Aristo, hesitates when his astrologer reminds him that it is an unlucky day. Against his better judgement he finally decides to go. Everything is ready at his farm by the Nile.

First reading. The language of this passage is straightforward. Once they have heard it in Latin, students could read it through individually or in pairs. Check their understanding with a series of questions, e.g.:

What did Barbillus invite Quintus and Aristo to?
What preparation did he make?
What did Phormio take with him? Why?
What caused Barbillus to hesitate?
Why did he decide to go ahead? Give two reasons.
Describe the scene at the farm.
Make a list of the jobs Phormio had carried out.

The presence of the astrologer will need an explanation. It was common for the wealthy to keep astrologers in their households and consult them about domestic and business matters. It was easy for them to become a powerful influence if their predictions proved correct.

Discussion

1 *Hunting* can be an emotive topic. Encourage the students to see it from the viewpoint of the ancient world. It developed a young man's strength, bravery, and skill with weapons, and it was useful in a society where every public career required military service and command in the Roman army; for some it was one of the few ways of obtaining meat. Why do you think Quintus was keen to proceed with this particular hunt?

2 *Astrology.* Ask students to think of a modern equivalent to the amulet. Discuss the continuing popularity of astrology. The serious scientific

study of astronomy in the ancient world, as well as the pseudo-science of astrology, was developed by a priestly caste from Babylonia known as the Chaldaeans. Elicit from students the difference between the two.

3 *Atmosphere*. This story leads to the death of Barbillus in Stage 20. Without revealing this, help the students to gain a sense of foreboding from: **perīculōsum est tibi** (lines 8–9), **Barbillus ... rem diū cōgitāvit** (lines 10–11), the irony underlying **sēcūrī** (line 14), and the slaughter of the young goats. Why were they killed?

Consolidation. The range of persons and tenses makes this passage useful for revising verbs. Ask the students to keep the passage in front of them and direct them to sentences or clauses, asking for a translation of the verb alone. Then use this verb as the basis for oral substitution exercises (see Book I Teacher's Guide, p. 16) before moving on to another sentence. If short of time, select ten verbs and test them quickly at the end of a lesson. The students write down their answers and mark their own work.

The incidence of verbs followed by a dative has been increasing during the last few Stages. This passage contains three examples: **appropinquat** (line 9), **crēdēbat** (line 11) and **persuādēre** (line 13). This would be a good opportunity to study these examples in conjunction with 'Language information' (p. 164).

Illustration. Detail of the Farnese Atlas, Hellenistic marble statue (*Naples, Archaeological Museum*).

vēnātiō II (p. 123)

Story. The hunters accidentally rouse a hippopotamus which overturns the boat carrying Barbillus and three slaves. The hunters drive away the crocodiles by throwing spears, but Barbillus is wounded in the shoulder.

First reading. Keep a lively pace in order to bring out the danger and excitement of the story, reading it with the class as far as **in aquam dēiēcit** (line 14), and leaving the students to discover the result for themselves by translating the last paragraph in groups of 3–4.

Discussion

1 *Style*. Lines 7–10 are the climax of the first part of this story. Who are the main participants? Can you devise a really stylish English translation for the sentence **magna erat fortitūdō ... Aethiopum** (lines 8–9)? Who does the writer suggest will win? Is that what actually happens?

2 *Barbillus' accident*. What was the cause? Taking into account the kind of wound Barbillus suffered, his spell in the water, his state of mind and the astrologer's warning, what do you think will happen to him?

Consolidation

1 Pick out the relative clauses and ask students to identify the noun being described, giving its gender and number, and then translate the sentence.
2 Ask the students to look back over **vēnātiō I** and **II** and select and translate three sentences which represent significant moments in the story.

Illustrations

- Amulet to ward off evil (*Naples, Archaeological Museum*), depicting hippopotamus goddess, moulded in 'Egyptian faience', a popular material made of a glaze on a moulded sandy core.
- Scenes of the Nile peopled by pygmies were popular in the Roman world (*Rome, Museo Nazionale*). In this mosaic do you find the animals lifelike? Do the hunters look as if they will overwhelm the animals? Is the overall impact of the mosaic comic, realistic or fanciful?

About the language 3: vocative case (p. 124)

New language feature. The vocative case.

Discussion. Work through paragraph 1 with the students. Ask them to study and translate the examples in paragraph 3 before discussing the different endings of the vocative and moving on to paragraph 4.

Consolidation. Exercises on the vocative can be found in *Independent Learning Manual* Stage 19. *Worksheet Master* 19.7 consists of a dramatic dialogue, entitled **fēminae Alexandrīnae**, which reinforces the vocative and imperative.

Illustration. Detail of wall-painting from temple of Isis at Pompeii, showing crocodile lurking in vegetation, lotus plants nearby, native reed-thatched hut in background, shrines in foreground.

Practising the language (p. 125)

Exercise 1. Complete the sentences by selecting the correct form of **hic** and **ille**, using the Vocabulary at the end of the book to check the gender of nouns if necessary.

Exercise 2. Recognise the case of an unfinished noun in the context of the sentences, and add the appropriate case ending, using the table of nouns in 'Language information' (pp. 150–1).

Language information: revision

Revisit nouns (pp. 150–2). Study the notes on p. 150 and work through exercises 7 and 8 on p. 152.

Revise adjectives (p. 153).

Work on 'Verbs with the dative' (p. 164) has already been indicated.

Cultural background material (pp. 126–9)

Content. The importance of Isis in Egyptian religion, her worship, her wider appeal in the Roman world.

Discussion

1 *The worship of Isis.* Isis, the mother goddess, gives life to the land and all its creatures, and hope of life after death. Help the students to build up a picture of how she was worshipped at the spring festival from the stories and the cultural background section, and gather details of daily worship from the illustration on p. 128 and from **Clēmēns tabernārius**, pp. 98–9. Some students may be able to compare the festival with modern religious celebrations in this country and in other parts of the world.

2 *Comparison of the worship of Isis with Christianity.* The cult of Isis spread through the Roman world at the same time as the spread of Christianity. There are similarities because the early Christian church tended to assimilate from other religions ideas and practices in tune with its own outlook. Students who are conversant with Christianity may be able to identify similarities, e.g.:

> Repentance, fasting and baptism.
> Hope of life after death.
> The Trinity and the linking of Isis, Osiris and Horus.
> Sacramental meals and private meditation as a way of communing with the godhead.
> The use of incense, flowers, light, music and choirs, and the adoration of relics.

Unlike Christianity, the cult of Isis did not survive. Possible reasons for this include:

> It was expensive to become a follower of Isis.
> There was no historical foundation for the myths about Isis, Osiris and Horus, and no well-defined set of beliefs.
> Isis worship did not require an ethical or moral commitment in daily life.
> It did not lead to concern about the welfare of other people and the principles of government.
> It lost its distinctive identity because it accommodated other gods.
> The demands of Christianity were uncompromising.

3 *Different religions today.* In some circumstances it may be possible for students to share their own diverse experiences.

Illustrations

p. 126 ● Sistra from Pompeii (*Naples, Archaeological Museum*). Sistra were shaken to repel the forces of evil or to express joy or mourning. The bronze rods jingle when shaken from side to side. Sometimes rattles are used in the modern orchestra.

- Woman playing sistrum; detail from mosaic of the seasons, Carthage, 4th century AD (*British Museum*), representing the month of November when the festival took place to celebrate the finding of Osiris' body.
- Statuette of Isis, 4th century BC (*British Museum*), wearing on her head her throne hieroglyph and (just visible underneath it) the **uraeus**, a rearing cobra which symbolised kingship.

p. 127
- Isis and her brother Osiris, relief with original painting, 13th century BC, from the temple of Seti I at Abydos, headquarters of the worship of Osiris. He wears the white crown of Upper Egypt adorned with feathers. Isis wears the horns and sun-disc of Hathor above a vulture head-dress.
- Bronze coin, 2nd century AD, from Alexandria (*British Museum*). Isis Pharia grasps the top corners of a square sail as it billows out before her. The Pharos shows the ramp leading up to the entrance, the statues of Tritons on the corners of the bottom storey, and the statue on the apex of the building.
- Detail of mosaic, showing the Nile flooding round a small island, about 80 BC (*Palestrina, Museo Prenestino Barberiniano*). Two men chat in the doorway of a reed hut while their companion watches the cow, and another rows a reed boat. Lotuses can be seen among the vegetation in the water, and ibises perch on the roof (*Photo Michael Holford*).

p. 128
- Wall-painting from Herculaneum, showing morning ceremony of Isis (*Naples, Archaeological Museum*). The temple at the top of the steps is flanked by palm trees and sphinxes crowned with lotus. The shaven-headed high priest in the doorway holds Nile water in a sacred vessel, ready to pour the morning libations on all the altars in the precinct; the priest and priestess beside him are shaking sistra; below them a priest with a wand conducts a choir of men and women; another priest fans the flames on a small horned altar garlanded with flowers, ready for the offering of milk, honey or herbs; a priest and priestess (front left) shake sistra; the standing priest (front right) carries a rod, the seated one plays a flute. A sacred ibis, symbol of healing, has settled on the back of the left-hand sphinx, two others wander in the foreground.

p. 129
- For the Egyptian Isis, see notes on opening page (p. 60 of this Guide).
- Isis welcoming Io to Egypt. Detail of wall-painting from temple of Isis in Pompeii (*Naples, Archaeological Museum*). The worship of Isis was established in Rome by the 1st century BC. Though periodically banned from the city itself, the cult was favoured by the Flavian emperors. It was virtually dead by the 4th century.

- Isis was the goddess of fruitfulness. In her temple in Pompeii were found fish and eggs as well as the walnuts, grain and bread shown here (*Photo Alinari*).

p. 130 • Model hippopotamus, made of 'Egyptian faience' (see note on amulet on p. 67 of this Guide) (*British Museum*).

Suggested activities

1 Read to the class extracts from the novel by Apuleius, *The Golden Ass* (Penguin), which deals with Isis in chapters 17–18.
2 Imagine that you are Clemens and tell Quintus why you are attracted to the worship of Isis.
3 Study the four Nile scenes (pp. 123, 124, 127 and 147), comparing them with the photograph of the Nile (p. 108), and answer the following questions:

What facts about the Nile can you deduce from the pictures?
What fantastic elements do you detect?
What do you think made these scenes so popular among the Romans of Italy?
Which scene do you prefer and why?

STAGE 20 medicus

Cultural background	Story line	Main language features	Focus of exercises
Alexandria: medicine, mathematics, astronomy, inventions.	Conflicting treatments, provided for Barbillus' shoulder by the Greek doctor and the astrologer, result in Barbillus' death. Quintus is asked to look for his son in Britain.	• Present participle. • **is** and **ea** in accusative, genitive and dative.	1 Present participle. 2 Imperative. 3 Relative clauses.

Opening page (p. 131)

Illustration. Sealstone made of sard, a kind of cornelian, Roman, 1st–2nd century AD, showing doctor (right) examining the swollen stomach of a standing youth. Asclepius, god of medicine (left), leans on his staff, around which his familiar serpent is coiled.

Model sentences (p. 132)

Story. Barbillus is carried to his bed. The astrologer bursts in while Phormio runs for a doctor.

New language feature. Present participle in the nominative case.

First reading. Students quickly work out how to translate the sentences correctly. As usual, postpone formal discussion until 'About the language' (p. 135).

Consolidation. Recapitulation of selected sentences at the beginning or end of the next few lessons will be necessary to establish the new form. Pave the way for the important notion of agreement by asking, for example, of sentence 1 '*Who* were carrying Barbillus?'

remedium astrologī (p. 133)

Story. Phormio tries in vain to staunch the blood with an improvised bandage, then with cobwebs. When the astrologer bursts in with recriminations, Barbillus asks Quintus to send for Petro the doctor.

First reading. At the start, **ego** reminds the reader that Quintus is telling the story. The first paragraph presents a challenge with the rapidly switching tenses. Students enjoy the impact of **sanguis** in the final position.

The next two sections of the story, **servī ... collocāvit** (lines 6–15) and

astrologus ancillās ... remedium est (lines 16–24), could be approached by the students on their own, in pairs or groups. The penultimate sentence **Phormiōnem ... ēmīsī** (line 29) often causes difficulty. Give help by reading it through to the end, eliciting the significance of word endings as you go. Reinforce this sentence pattern with other examples the students have already met, e.g. **servum, quī tam fortis ... fuerat, līberāvī** (Stage 16, p. 67, line 8).

Help the class to appreciate the suspense of the final section, and the contrasting purposes of the steward and the astrologer, which the writer emphasises by the word order of the last sentence.

Discussion

1 *Focus of story.* Why do you think the writer has given the story this title? How does it relate to the last two words of the passage? Is he being ironic?
2 *The astrologer.* Do you agree with the astrologer that his earlier warnings have been proved right?
3 *Quintus.* In what tone of voice did Quintus ask **habēsne remedium** (line 19)? What was his previous attitude to the astrologer? Has it changed? Refer back if necessary to **vēnātiō** (p. 122, line 10).
4 *Barbillus.* What do you think Barbillus' attitude to the astrologer is now?

Consolidation. Give further practice with familiar examples of any sentence patterns that have caused problems. Then ask the class to write a good translation of the first and last paragraphs.

Illustration. Detail from mosaic representing unswept floor of dining-room (*Rome, Vatican Museums*). Another detail is illustrated in Book I (p. 87).

Petrō (p. 134)

Story. After trouncing the astrologer, the Greek doctor cleans and stitches Barbillus' wound, and advises quiet and rest. Quintus stays to help Barbillus with his business affairs, and learns his sad story.

First reading. Guide the students through the story by the use of lively Latin reading and comprehension questions.

Discussion. Students are usually fascinated by the medical practices described in these stories. The homely remedies of Phormio, the slave-doctor, are derived from Celsus, a medical writer in the 1st century AD, who gives a list of coagulants which includes cobwebs (in fact, the protein they contain deters gangrene). After the superstitious practices of the astrologer, this story emphasises the scientific competence of Petro: he knows the importance of hygiene, demonstrates surgical skill, and appreciates that healing is a natural process. Vinegar is used here as an antiseptic. Barbillus faints from shock. Combine this discussion with a study of pp. 142–4.

Consolidation. Ask the students to re-read one passage from the story, e.g. **mē ita … afflīxerat** (line 20–end), raising any queries or uncertainties they have. Then ask for an oral translation of selected sentences. Students could also list the things Petro does in lines 7–19 and write down which ones are good medical practice.

There are useful exercises in *Independent Learning Manual* Stage 20, and *Worksheet Master* 20.4.

Illustration. Petro stitching the wound.

About the language 1: present participles (p. 135)

New language feature. Present participle in nominative and accusative cases.

Discussion. Work through the three explanatory paragraphs with the class. If the students work at paragraph 4 on their own, you can go round identifying any problems requiring further help.

Consolidation. Ask the students to identify the present participles in the model sentences and say which noun each describes. *Worksheet Master* 20.1 has additional examples.

**fortūna crūdēlis (pp. 136–7)

Story. Barbillus' son persuades his mother to accompany him on a voyage to Greece, against the advice of the astrologer. The ship is wrecked and she is drowned. Barbillus refuses to have his son back.

First reading. A good approach to the story, for students in groups of 3, is provided by *Independent Learning Manual* Stage 20.

Discussion

1 *Family conflict.* This subject needs sensitive handling, but students may be interested to discuss in small groups the ethical problems presented here. Have they had similar disagreements? Would they have acted differently? Would they have wheedled concessions from a parent in the way that Rufus worked on his mother? Would they have been as successful? Did Rufus get what he deserved? Was Barbillus' reaction justified?

2 *Sailing in the Mediterranean.* Remind the students of the significance of the Spring festival of Isis, when the seaways re-opened to traffic and trade after almost total closure in the winter months. Some students may be able to relate first-hand encounters with the sudden storms characteristic of the Mediterranean. Shipwreck played a significant part in ancient literature, e.g.: the *Odyssey*, the *Aeneid*, and Paul's journey to his trial in Rome (Acts 27).

Consolidation. Ask the students to complete the comprehension questions in writing. The answers and mark scheme are as follows. Give credit for any sensible answer.

		Marks
1	Plotina was faithful and calm; she contentedly stayed at home.	3
2	Rufus often went to the palaestra; he regularly hunted wild beasts.	2
3	He sometimes had rows with his parents, but they were very fond of each other.	2
4	Eupor was studying medicine.	1
5	(Soon) after his return to Athens.	1
	A wedding invitation to Rufus and his parents.	2
6	Barbillus was frightened to set sail because winter was now approaching.	2
7	The astrologer replied that they were undertaking a dangerous mission. The moon was already entering Scorpio. It would be safer for them to stay at home.	3
8	Rufus wanted to go to the wedding/to see his friend again/to travel abroad.	1
	(When his father was away) he often went to his mother and complained about his father.	2
9	He persuaded Plotina, but he could not persuade his father.	2
10	A huge storm overwhelmed it.	1
	Rufus was able to swim to the shore; Plotina was drowned.	2
11	Barbillus refused to see Rufus again. (Although he wished to return home) Rufus obeyed his father.	2
	Rufus went to Britain where he served in the Roman army.	2
12	*Yes,* Rufus was right because astrology is mumbo-jumbo. The shipwreck was a sheer accident (although more likely in the winter).	
	Or:	
	No, Rufus was wrong. The astrologer was sensible to warn Barbillus of the danger of sailing in the winter (although his belief in astrology may have been misguided).	2

TOTAL 30

Illustration. Mosaic of merchant ship, late 2nd century (*Tunisia, Sousse Museum*). The ship is driven by oars as well as the wind. A decorative dolphin projects at the prow. Ribbons are hung on the mast and above the helmsman's reed cabin at the stern to indicate the direction of the wind. The vessel has eyes, either to see the way or to ward off the evil eye, a feature seen on many Mediterranean boats today.

About the language 2: eum, eam, etc. (p. 138)

New language feature. The accusative, genitive and dative cases of **is** and **ea**, in the singular and the plural.

Discussion. After studying the explanation and the examples, pick out instances from the stories, and ask the students to translate them in their context, e.g.:

servī … eum lēniter posuērunt (p. 133, lines 6–7).
Petrō … ad vīllam eius festīnāvit (p. 134, lines 1–2).
eam in vulnus collocāvit (p. 134, line 8).
necesse est eī … (p. 134, line 21).
negōtium eius administrāns (p. 134, line 25).
fortūna eum … afflīxerat (p. 134, line 29).
nāvis, quae eōs vehēbat … (p. 136, line 26).
tempestās eam obruit (p. 136, line 27).

If you elicit from the students that some of the corresponding English pronouns, *he, him, his, they, them, their*, etc. are among the few English words to possess cases, they are more likely to see the inflections as a 'natural' feature of language.

Consolidation. When making up further examples, give the students a preliminary sentence to establish the context. If you give students English sentences containing pronouns and ask them to translate the pronoun, allow them to use the table on p. 138 initially and then see if they can manage without it.

astrologus victor I (pp. 138–9)

Story. The astrologer visits Barbillus on his sickbed and tries to undermine his confidence in the doctor with slanderous statements about his poor record and his greed for money. Barbillus refuses to listen.

First reading. After hearing the passage read in Latin, the students should be able to translate it in pairs or groups. Afterwards, you could check their understanding by putting some questions on the board for them to answer in writing, e.g.:

1 Which sentence shows how the astrologer and Petro felt about each other?
2 Can you give the Latin word which is the opposite of **inimīcī** (line 2)?
3 Translate the sentence **ad cubiculum … veniēbat** (lines 6–7).
4 Make a list of the lies the astrologer tells about Petro.
5 What had Petro done to excite such hatred? If necessary, refer the students to page 134 (lines 4–6).
6 What instruction of the astrologer made Barbillus **anxius** (line 13)?
7 Why did the astrologer hatch a plot?
8 What do you think he plans to do?

Consolidation

1 Ask the students to read aloud in Latin the astrologer's speech to Barbillus with appropriate expression. A written translation of line 9–end in appropriate English could be set for homework.
2 Reinforcement of comparatives and superlatives could be undertaken in connection with lines 9–11. See 'Language information' (pp. 154–5).
3 For students on short courses, there is a quick method of completing **astrologus victor I** and **II** in *Independent Learning Manual* Stage 20.

astrologus victor II (p. 139)

Story. The astrologer says that, in a dream, the young slave who was killed in the riot has given him a special remedy, and so Barbillus allows the astrologer to treat him. The wound deteriorates, the astrologer flees, and Barbillus gives Quintus his final message for his son.

First reading. Take the students through the first part of the passage, as far as **ad cubiculum arcessīvit** (line 13), giving help as necessary. The astrologer's speech presents a challenge because of the absence of nominatives from many sentences. The rest of the story could be read in groups or pairs.

Discussion

1 *Beliefs about astrology.* What is it that makes Barbillus believe in the astrologer? Encourage the students to recall his predictions in **vēnātiō** (p. 122, lines 8–9) and **fortūna crūdēlis** (p. 136, lines 16–17). Why do you think Barbillus refuses to recall Petro?
2 *Letter to Rufus.* What do you think this contained?
3 *Responsibility.* Who was ultimately to blame for Barbillus' death?

Consolidation. Ask the students to identify all the dative cases in the passage and translate the sentences containing them.

Illustration. Papyrus letter (*British Museum*) reads:
Prokleios to his good friend Pekysis greetings. You will do well if, at your own risk, you sell to my friend Sotas such high-quality goods as he will tell you he needs, for him to bring to me at Alexandria. Know that you will have to deal with me about the cost. Greet all your family from me. Farewell.

Practising the language (pp. 140–1)

Exercise 1. Complete the sentences with the correct form of present participle, selecting between nominative and accusative, singular and plural. This exercise is demanding. Help students by asking 'What noun does the participle describe? What is the case/number of that noun? Which then is the matching participle?'
Exercise 2. Complete the sentences with the correct form of the imperative.

Exercise 3. Translation passage practising the relative clause. It will help students to recognise clause boundaries if you first read them the passage in Latin. Remind them that the punctuation and the position of the relative pronoun and the verb usually help them to recognise where clauses begin and end.

Illustration. Head of young man, in wax, egg and oil on limewood, AD 80–120, from Hawara (*British Museum*). He is shown naked, which suggests a life devoted to exercise in the Greek gymnasium.

Language information: revision

The comparative and superlative of adjectives (pp. 154–5) can conveniently be revised after reading **astrologus victor I** (pp. 138–9). Revise 'Pronouns II' (p. 158) augmented by examples drawn from stories. Students could be divided into groups and set to hunt the pronouns in different stories. When found, the pronouns should be presented and translated in the context of the sentence. 'Longer sentences II' (p. 169) should be completed by the end of this Stage to help students appreciate these sentence patterns, which often cause problems, and translate them fluently.

Cultural background material (pp. 142–5)

Content. The section about medicine is best studied in conjunction with **Petrō** (p. 134). The further information about mathematics, astronomy and engineering could be compared with the pseudo-science of astrology as demonstrated in the stories.

Discussion

1 *Science and superstition.* How can advanced scientific knowledge co-exist with a belief in astrology? Do you find these stories convincing? Are there modern parallels?
2 *The Hippocratic oath.* What problems confront modern doctors in following these principles? Relevant ethical issues include confidentiality, euthanasia, abortion, the use of injections for the death penalty in the United States.

Illustrations

p. 142 • For sealstone, see note on opening page, p. 71 of this Guide.
  • Terracotta model of internal organs, 3rd–1st century BC (*British Museum*), dedicated either in hope of, or in gratitude for, a cure.
p. 143 • Relief of medical instruments, time of Trajan, temple at Komombo on the Nile.
  • Bleeding cup, bronze (*British Museum*). Celsus, writing in the 1st century AD, explains that burning lint was placed inside the vessel which was then applied over an incision in the skin. The vacuum drew the blood into the cup.

p. 144
- Set of Roman surgical instruments, 1st century AD (*British Museum*), found together in Italy. Top row from left: catheters, rectal speculum. Middle row from left: instrument cases, 3 spatulae for mixing and applying ointment, 6 scoops and spoons, 8 probes, forceps and hooks, 1 double-ended traction hook, 2 bone chisels. Bottom row from left: palette for grinding medicines, 2 + 4 spatulae with a folding knife below, 5 handles for scalpels of which the blades have rusted away; the oval ends (at right) are blunt dissectors for pushing apart the incision.
- Roman bonesaw in bronze, 1st–3rd century AD (*British Museum*).
- Oculist's stamp, 1st–3rd century AD (*British Museum*). The remedies include 'saffron ointment for soreness' and 'saffron ointment for scratches and running eyes, prepared by Junius Taurus from a prescription of Pacius'.
- Diagram of Eratosthenes' experiment.

p. 145
- Part of astronomical treatise called *The Art of Eudoxus*, first half of 2nd century BC, found in the temple of Serapis (*Louvre, photo Réunion des Musées Nationaux*).
- Diagram of Hero's steam turbine.

p. 146
- The pyramids of Gizeh outside Cairo. From left to right: the tombs of Khufu (140m high), Khephren and Menkaure, 3rd millennium BC.

Suggested activities

1 The teacher could write the following epigram from Martial (I.47) on the board or OHP and help the students to read and appreciate it. Some may like to attempt a verse translation, perhaps in limerick form. They might then discuss whether such jokes were justified, or try writing another of their own, or compare English jokes about doctors.

> nūper erat medicus, nunc est vespillo Diaulus;
>   quod vespillo facit, fēcerat et medicus.   [vespillo *undertaker*]
> *On Diaulus: Previously a doctor, presently an undertaker,*
>   *What he does in his new job, he used to do in his old.*

2 Make out a list of the medical treatments described in the background material and say which would be effective.

3 With a group of friends, make a list of modern scientific developments you think are based upon research in ancient Alexandria. Select the one you consider most important in today's world. Explain to the class, with illustrations, the modern development you have chosen, why it is important, and the original discovery that made it possible. Invite your science and technology teachers to attend your presentation and comment.

4 Draw or make a model of one of the Alexandrian inventions and demonstrate it to the class. Invite your science and technology teachers to attend your presentation.
5 Set Attainment test 3 (pp. 85–8 of this Guide) to assess students' progress at the end of this Book.

Other illustrations

Language information (p. 147). Detail, mosaic of a Nile scene, from House of the Faun, Pompeii (*Naples, Archaeological Museum*).
Front cover. 'Gayer-Anderson' cat, front view (see note on p. 56 of this Guide). It sits (unhistorically) on a mosaic from Fishbourne (see note on p. 41 of this Guide).
Back cover. Mosaic of a merchant ship (see note on p. 74 of this Guide).

LANGUAGE SYNOPSIS OF BOOK II

This synopsis follows the same plan and is designed for the same purposes as the Book I language synopsis described on p. 92 of the Book I Teacher's Guide. When reading a Stage with a class, teachers are strongly advised to concentrate on the features dealt with in that Stage's language note(s), rather than attempting discussion and analysis of other features listed here. LI = Language information section.

Stage	Language feature	Place of language note, etc.
13	infinitive + **volō, nōlō, possum**	13
	present tense of **volō, nōlō, possum**	13, LI
	-que	13
	perfect passive participle	21
	clauses with **quamquam** and **simulac**	LI
	nominative singular of 2nd declension neuter nouns	LI
	omission of verb in second of two clauses	LI
	clauses with **ubi** (= *when*)	LI
	sēcum	LI
	apposition (nominative)	
	nominative predicative adjective	
14	attributive adjective (met from Stage 3): agreement of case and number	14, LI
	infinitive + **decōrum, difficile**, etc.	
	vocative in **-ī**	19, LI
	nōlī (one example)	19
	imperative plural (one example)	19
	present participle	20
	ipse	
	apposition (accusative)	
	accusative predicative adjective	
15	relative clauses with nominative singular and plural and accusative singular of **quī**	15, LI
	imperfect of **possum, volō, nōlō**	15, LI
	infinitive + **dēbeō**	
	appropinquō + dative	LI
	omission of verb in first of two clauses (one example)	LI
16	pluperfect (in relative clause)	16
	infinitive + **audeō**	

Stage	Language feature	Place of language note, etc.
	relative clauses with accusative plural of **quī**	
	relative clauses in sentences with subject omitted	
17	genitive singular and plural (in prepositional phrases)	17, LI
	obstō + dative	LI
	DATIVE + VERB word order	LI
	increased incidence of VERB + NOMINATIVE word order (from Stage 3)	LI
	increased complexity in subordinate clauses	LI
	pluperfect in main clause	
	infinitive + **soleō, coepī, melius est**	
18	adjective (met from Stage 3): agreement of gender	18, LI
	increased incidence of verbs with dative	LI
	genitive + nominative (one example)	LI
	genitive + accusative (one example)	LI
	omission of verb in first of two clauses (met in Stage 15)	LI
	DATIVE + ACCUSATIVE + VERB word order	LI
	ACCUSATIVE + NOMINATIVE + VERB word order	LI
	ACCUSATIVE + VERB + NOMINATIVE word order	LI
	'nesting' of one subordinate clause inside another (e.g. **ubi ā templō, in quō cēnāverat, domum redībat, amīcum cōnspexit accurrentem**)	
	ACCUSATIVE + DATIVE + VERB word order	
	clauses with **ut** (= *as*)	
19	genitive + nominative and accusative (from Stage 18)	LI
	genitive of adjective	LI
	hic (met from Stage 8)	19, LI
	ille (met from Stage 9)	19, LI
	imperative singular (from Stage 10) and plural (from Stage 14)	19, LI
	nōlī (from Stage 14) and **nōlīte**	19
	vocative (from Stages 11 and 14)	19, LI
	fīō + predicative nominative	
20	present participle (met from Stage 14)	20
	oblique cases of **is** (from Stage 7)	20, LI
	descriptive genitive (one example)	22
	'stringing' arrangement of 2 parallel subordinate clauses (e.g. **servī, quī Barbillum portābant, ubi cubiculum intrāvērunt, in lectum eum lēniter posuērunt**)	
	increased incidence of predicative adjective	

The following terms are used in Book II. Numerals indicate the Stage in which each term is first used. LI = Language information section.

Term	Stage
infinitive	13
adjective	14
agree(ment)	14
number	14
relative clause	15
pluperfect	16
genitive	17
gender	18
masculine	18
feminine	18
neuter	18
imperative	19
vocative	19
present participle	20
pronoun	LI
relative pronoun	LI
antecedent	LI
1st, 2nd, 3rd person	LI

APPENDIX A: ATTAINMENT TESTS

For notes on the purpose of the attainment tests, and suggestions for their use, see the Book I Teacher's Guide, p. 95. The words and phrases in bold type are either new to students or have occurred infrequently in the reading material.

Test 1

To be given at the end of Stage 16. Translate the title for the students before reading the story aloud to them.

somnium mīrābile

Sextus et Titus erant amīcī. ad urbem **iter faciēbant**. postquam ad urbem pervēnērunt, Sextus ad tabernam contendit. Titus tamen apud frātrem manēbat. post cēnam Titus, quod fessus erat, mox obdormīvit. subitō Sextus in **somniō** appāruit.

'amīce!' inquit. '**caupō** mē necāre vult. necesse est tibi mē **adiuvāre.'** 5
Titus statim surrēxit, quod **commōtus** erat, et sibi dīxit,
'num caupō amīcum meum necāre vult? minimē! somnium erat.'
Titus iterum obdormīvit. Sextus iterum in somniō appāruit.
'ēheu!' inquit. 'mortuus sum. caupō **scelestus** mē necāvit. postquam mē
necāvit, in **plaustrō** mē **cēlāvit**. tū eum pūnīre dēbēs.' 10
Titus ē lectō perterritus surrēxit. ad **vigilēs** festīnāvit remque nārrāvit.
tum cum duōbus vigilibus ad tabernam contendit. caupōnem rogāvit,
'ubi est Sextus, amīcus meus, quī in hāc tabernā manēbat?'
'**errōrem** facis', caupō eī respondit. '**nēmō** est in tabernā.'
Titus, ubi plaustrum in viā cōnspexit, clāmāvit, 15
'ecce! amīcus meus, quem tū necāvistī, in hōc plaustrō **cēlātus** est.'
vigilēs, postquam plaustrum īnspexērunt, Sextum invēnērunt mortuum.
caupōnem attonitum **comprehendērunt**, et eum ad **iūdicem** dūxērunt.

Test 2

To be given at the end of Stage 18, preferably in two successive lessons. Translate the title for the students before reading the Latin aloud.

ad pȳramidas

I

ōlim Quīntus ad tabernam Clēmentis contendit. ubi ad tabernam pervēnit, Clēmentem salūtāvit.
'salvē, amīce', inquit. 'ego tibi aliquid dīcere volō. ad **pȳramidas** iter facere cupiō. sunt enim in Aegyptō multae pȳramides quās Aegyptiī ōlim **exstrūxērunt**. Aegyptiī in pȳramidibus rēgēs **sepelīre** solēbant. ego 5 pȳramidas vidēre volō quod sunt maximae et pulcherrimae. vīsne mēcum iter facere?'

Clēmēns laetus cōnsēnsit. itaque Quīntus et Clēmēns pecūniam cibumque in **saccīs** posuērunt. tum ad Plūtum, mercātōrem Graecum, festīnāvērunt et **camēlōs condūxērunt**. saccōs, quōs ē tabernā Clēmentis portāverant, in camēlīs posuērunt. tum camēlōs **cōnscendērunt** et ex urbe discessērunt. per agrōs et vīllās prōcēdēbant.   10

subitō decem Aegyptiī, quī **īnsidiās** parāverant, **impetum** fēcērunt. Quīntus et Clēmēns fortiter resistēbant sed facile erat Aegyptiīs eōs superāre quod fūstēs ingentēs habēbant. tum Aegyptiī cum pecūniā et   15
camēlīs effūgērunt. Quīntus et Clēmēns trīstēs ad urbem reveniēbant.

'ēheu!' inquit Clēmēns. 'quam miserī sumus! pȳramidas nōn vīdimus; pecūniam camēlōsque āmīsimus.'

II

When you have read this part of the story, answer the questions at the end.

Quīntus et Clēmēns per urbem fessī prōcēdēbant. ubi tabernam Plūtī **praeterībant**, rem mīrābilem vīdērunt. camēlī, quōs Aegyptiī **abdūxerant**, **extrā** tabernam Plūtī stābant! tum Quīntus rem tōtam intellēxit. amīcī īrātī mercātōrem quaesīvērunt, sed invenīre nōn poterant. aderat tamen puer parvus quī camēlōs custōdiēbat. Quīntus clāmāvit,   5

'heus, puer! ubi sunt Aegyptiī quī in nōs impetum fēcērunt? ego eōs dē pecūniā meā **interrogāre** volō.'

puer perterritus

'rogā Plūtum', inquit, et statim fūgit.

amīcī per viās Alexandrīae Plūtum frūstrā quaesīvērunt. tandem portuī   10
appropinquāvērunt. ecce! Plūtus cum **duōbus** Aegyptiīs negōtium agēbat. Quīntus hominēs agnōvit. eōs enim vīderat in turbā Aegyptiōrum quī impetum fēcerant. Quīntus ad Plūtum prōcessit, quī, postquam eum īrātum vīdit, valdē timēbat.

'ubi est mea pecūnia?' inquit Quīntus. 'camēlōs iam invēnimus!'   15

Plūtus erat perterritus quod Quīntus erat cīvis Rōmānus. Plūtus Quīntō **'ignōsce** mihi', inquit. 'decōrum est mihi pecūniam reddere. dōnum quoque tibi offerre volō.'

deinde Quīntum et Clēmentem ad vīllam suam dūxit. ibi eīs duōs equōs dedit. Quīntus numquam equōs pulchriōrēs quam illōs vīderat. tum   20
Quīntus et Clēmēns equōs cōnscendērunt et ad pȳramidas laetī contendērunt.

Questions

1 Which Latin word describes how Quintus and Clemens were feeling (line 1)? Translate it.   1
2 Explain what the **rem mīrābilem** (line 2) was.   2
3 When Quintus realised what had happened, what did the friends do? How successful were they (lines 3–4)?   2
4 What was the little boy doing (lines 4–5)?   1

5 What question did Quintus ask him?   2
6 What did the boy do that showed he was **perterritus**?   1
7 Where was Plutus when Quintus and Clemens found him?
   What was he doing (lines 10–11)?   2
8 Why did Quintus recognise the men (lines 12–13)?   2
9 Why was Plutus terrified when Quintus told him about the
   camels (line 16)?   1
10 How did Plutus propose to put things right (lines 17–18)?   2
11 **duōs equōs** (line 19). Why did they impress Quintus?   2
12 How does the story end?   2

TOTAL 20

Answers

The answers and mark scheme are as follows. Give credit for any sensible
answer.
1 **fessī**; tired   1
2 The camels, which the Egyptians had taken away, were
   standing outside Plutus' shop.   2
3 They looked for the merchant. Unsuccessful; they could not
   find him.   2
4 The little boy was guarding the camels.   1
5 Quintus asked him where were the Egyptians who had
   attacked them.   2
6 He ran away.   1
7 At/near the harbour. Plutus was doing business with two
   Egyptians.   2
8 They had been in the crowd of Egyptians who had attacked
   him.   2
9 Quintus was a Roman citizen.   1
10 He would return the money and offer Quintus a present.   2
11 Quintus had never seen finer horses than those.   2
12 Quintus and Clemens mounted the horses and happily
   hastened to the pyramids.   2

TOTAL 20

Test 3

To be given at the end of Stage 20, preferably in two successive lessons.
Translate the title for the students before reading the Latin aloud.

testāmentum Barbillī

I

multī amīcī cum Galatēā et Aristōne cēnābant. dē morte Barbillī **sermōnem**
habēbant.

    'magnum **lēgātum** exspectō', inquit Galatēa. 'nam ubi Barbillus aeger

iacēbat, eum cotīdiē vīsitābam. magnam partem diēī cum eō
cōnsūmēbam.'

    omnēs Galatēam laudāvērunt et clāmāvērunt,
    'decōrum est tibi praemium accipere.'

    Petrō, medicus Graecus, triclīnium intrāvit. Galatēa, ubi eum cōnspexit,
īrāta surrēxit.

    'cūr hūc vēnistī?' inquit. 'nōs omnēs tē **dēspicimus**, quod tū Barbillum
sānāre nōn poterās.'

    'ego hūc vēnī, quod tibi aliquid dīcere volō', respondit Petrō.

    'quid est?' rogāvit Galatēa.

    '**testāmentum** Barbillī vīdī', respondit ille.

    Galatēa, ubi hoc audīvit, **īram dēposuit**. Petrōnem in mediōs amīcōs
dūxit et cibum vīnumque eī obtulit.

    'ō **dulcissime**', inquit Galatēa, 'quam libenter tē vidēmus. **dīc** nōbīs
quam celerrimē dē testāmentō! quid Barbillus nōbīs relīquit?'

5

10

15

II

When you have read this part of the story, answer the questions at the end.

omnēs tacuērunt et Petrōnem intentē audīvērunt.

    'Barbillus Aristōnī nūllam pecūniam relīquit', inquit Petrō, 'sed
tragoediās, quās Aristō scrīpsit, reddidit.'

    amīcī, ubi hoc audīvērunt, valdē rīsērunt quod tragoediae Aristōnis
pessimae erant. Galatēa quoque rīsit.

    'optimē fēcit Barbillus', inquit Galatēa. 'Barbillus Aristōnī tragoediās
sōlum relīquit quod Aristō nihil aliud cūrat. **sine dubiō** Barbillus mihi
multam pecūniam relīquit quod ego sapientior sum quam marītus meus.'

    tum Petrō Galatēae dīxit,

    'Barbillus fīliae tuae **gemmās** pretiōsās, quās ā mercātōre **Syriō** ēmerat,
relīquit.'

    'quam fortūnāta est Helena!' exclāmāvērunt amīcī.

    Galatēa hanc rem graviter ferēbat.

    'nōn decōrum est Helenae gemmās habēre. nam Helena est stultior
quam pater. **tūtius est** Helenae gemmās mihi trādere. sed cūr nihil dē mē
dīcis, Petrō? quid Barbillus mihi relīquit?'

    Petrō tamen nihil respondit.

    Galatēa īrāta
    'dīc mihi, stultissime', inquit.

    tandem Petrō susurrāvit,
    'nihil tibi relīquit.'

    omnēs amīcī valdē commōtī erant: multī cachinnāvērunt, paucī
lacrimāvērunt.

    Galatēa tamen tacēbat. **humī** dēciderat exanimāta.

5

10

15

20

Questions

1 What did Aristo receive in the will?   1
2 What did Galatea's friends do when they heard what Aristo
   had received? Why did they do this?   2
3 What reason did Galatea give for Barbillus' legacy to Aristo
   (lines 6–7)?   2
4 What did Galatea hope to receive herself? Why?   2
5 Describe what Barbillus left to Helena (lines 10–11).   2
6 What were the different reactions of the friends and Galatea
   to Helena's legacy (lines 12–13)?   2
7 What did Galatea think about her daughter's character?   1
8 What did she think her daughter should do?   1
9 What did Galatea receive?   1
10 **omnēs amīcī valdē commōtī erant** (line 22). How did the
   friends show their feelings?   2
11 What was Galatea's reaction? Why was this (line 24)?   2
12 Look back over the story. How does Petro show his
   embarrassment about telling Galatea what she had received?
   Make two points.   2
                                                             TOTAL 20

Answers

The answers and mark scheme are as follows. Give credit for any sensible
answer.

1 His own tragedies/the tragedies which he had written.   1
2 They laughed a lot because Aristo's tragedies were very bad.   2
3 She said Barbillus had left only the tragedies to Aristo because
   he cared for nothing else.   2
4 Galatea hoped to receive a lot of money because she was wiser
   than her husband.   2
5 Barbillus left Helena precious jewels which he had bought
   from a Syrian merchant.   2
6 The friends thought Helena was lucky; Galatea took the news badly. 2
7 Galatea thought Helena was more stupid than her father.   1
8 She thought Helena should hand the jewels over to her.   1
9 Nothing.   1
10 Many laughed/roared with laughter; a few cried.   2
11 Galatea was silent. She had fainted/fallen unconscious on the
   ground.   2
12 *Two of:*
   Petro reported all the other legacies first/When Galatea asked
   him what Barbillus had left her, he did not answer/When she
   got angry and asked him again, he answered in a whisper.   2
                                                             TOTAL 20

Part I of this test can be used to assess, amongst other things, students' ability to handle the 1st and 2nd person inflections of the verb in various tenses. The teacher may also wish to note how they cope with the omission of the subject in **Petrōnem ... dūxit et cibum ... obtulit** (lines 15–16). If students produce *the will which Barbillus has left us* for line 18, discussion of the punctuation of the Latin may give them a clearer understanding of where they went wrong than analysis of the difference between **quid** and **quod**.

Vocabulary tested in Part II includes **rīdēre** (cf. question 2), **nihil aliud** (question 3), **emere** (question 5), **paucī** (question 10) and **tacēbat** (question 11). In answering question 12, students have not only to understand the text but also to draw inferences from it; such exploration of the text could be taken further in oral discussion after the test has been completed. For example, the class might be asked to pick out, and suggest explanations for, Galatea's change of tone from **ō dulcissime** (Part I, line 17) to **dīc mihi, stultissime** (Part II, line 19).

APPENDIX B:
BOOK II VOCABULARY CHECKLIST

The numeral indicates the Stage in whose checklist the word or phrase occurs. Verbs are shown here in their infinitive form for consistency with the corresponding lists in the Teacher's Guides to later Books.

ā, ab (= *from*) (17)
adīre (20)
advenīre (13)
aedificāre (16)
aedificium (13)
aeger (13)
agmen (15)
aliquid (14)
alius (15)
alter (13)
amāre (19)
animus (17)
appropinquāre (17)
apud (14)
aqua (15)
āra (17)
arcessere (20)
ars (20)
attonitus (14)
audēre (18)
aula (14)
auxilium (16)

bene (17)
benignus (17)
bonus (16)

cantāre (13)
caput (18)
cārus (19)
cēterī (13)
claudere (15)
coepisse (18)
cōgitāre (19)
cognōscere (18)
commodus (15)
comparāre (19)
cōnficere (19)
cōnsentīre (16)
cōnsilium (16)
cotīdiē (14)
crūdēlis (20)
cūrāre (19)
custōs (13)

dea (18)
dēbēre (15)
decem (20)
decōrus (14)
deinde (16)
dēlectāre (16)
dēlēre (14)
dēmōnstrāre (18)
dēnique (20)

dēspērāre (20)
deus (14)
dīcere (13)
difficilis (14)
dīligenter (14)
discēdere (18)
diū (17)
doctus (20)
domina (14)
domus (20)
dōnum (14)
duo (12, 20)

effugere (16)
equus (15)
etiam (15)
excitāre (13)

faber (17)
facilis (17)
fessus (13)
fidēlis (14)
fīlia (19)
flōs (16)
fluere (19)
fortasse (18)
forte (19)

grātiās agere (19)
graviter (17)

hasta (19)
hūc (17)

ibi (18)
illūc (19)
impedīre (15)
imperātor (16)
īnferre (20)
īnsula (17)
inter (16)
interficere (13)
invītus (17)
ipse (14)
iste (14)
ita (16)
ita vērō (13)
itaque (17)
iter (19)

lectus (15)
lentē (15)
libenter (18)
līberāre (20)
lītus (15)

locus (19)

lūna (20)

māne (19)

manus (= *hand*) (18)

mare (15)

marītus (14)

maximus (17)

melior (16)

mīles (18)

miser (15)

mors (20)

nam (18)

nauta (15)

nāvigāre (16)

necesse (14)

negōtium (17)

nēmō (18)

nōlle (13)

nōnne? (16)

novem (20)

nōvisse (19)

novus (13)

nūllus (13)

num? (14)

numquam (17)

obstāre (18)

octō (20)

oculus (20)

pars (18)

paucī (17)

perīculum (19)

perīre (16)

persuādēre (20)

pervenīre (17)

pessimus (20)

petere (= *beg for*)
  (18)

plūrimī (19)

pōnere (16)

poscere (19)

posse (13)

posteā (18)

postrīdiē (16)

prīnceps (15)

prō (18)

pūnīre (16)

quadrāgintā (20)

quam (= *how*) (14)

quamquam (14)

quattuor (20)

-que (14)

quī (15)

quīnquāgintā (20)

quīnque (20)

quō? (18)

quondam (17)

recipere (17)

recūsāre (18)

redīre (15)

relinquere (20)

resistere (17)

rēx (14)

ruere (13)

sacerdōs (15)

sē (13)

septem (20)

sex (20)

sīcut (20)

simulac (16)

solēre (18)

summus (16)

tam (20)

temptāre (20)

tenēre (15)

tollere (16)

tot (19)

trahere (13)

trēs (12, 20)

trīgintā (20)

ubi (= *when*) (14)

unda (15)

ūnus (12, 20)

velle (13)

vertere (16)

vexāre (19)

vīgintī (20)

vincere (15)

vīta (13)

vīvere (19)

vix (19)

vōx (19)

vulnerāre (13)

vulnus (20)

BIBLIOGRAPHY

Books

The following is a select bibliography on Roman Britain, Alexandria and other themes relevant to this Book. Some of the recommended books are out of print (OP) but are included in case teachers already possess them or can obtain second-hand copies. Books marked * are suitable for students.

General

Balsdon, J.P.V.D. *Life and Leisure in Ancient Rome* (Bodley Head, 1969, OP)

Cambridge Ancient History, Vol. X, 43 BC–AD 69 (Cambridge UP, new edn, 1996)

Freeman, C. *Egypt, Greece and Rome – Civilisations of the Ancient Mediterranean* (Oxford UP, 1996)

Grant, M. **Routledge Atlas of Classical History* (Routledge, 1994)

Hill, S. and Ireland, S. *Roman Britain* (Bristol Classical Press, 1996)

Jones, P. and Sidwell, K. *The World of Rome* (Cambridge UP, 1997)

Lewis, N. and Reinhold, M. (eds) *Roman Civilisation: A Sourcebook. II The Empire* (Columbia UP, new edn, 1990)

McEvedy, C. **Penguin Atlas of Ancient History* (Penguin, new edn, 1986)

Paoli, U.E. *Rome, Its People, Life and Customs* (Bristol Classical Press, 1990)

The Celts

James, S. and Rigby, R. *Britain and the Celtic Iron Age* (British Museum Publications, 1997)

Martell, H.M. **The Celts* (Hamlyn, 1995)

Rankin, D. *Celts and the Classical World* (Routledge, 1996)

Stead, I. *Celtic Art* (British Museum Publications, new edn, 1997)

Roman Britain

Andrews, I. **Boudicca's Revolt* (Cambridge UP, 1972, OP)

Cambridge School Classics Project **The Romans Discover Britain* and *Teacher's Handbook* (Cambridge UP, 1981)
   **The Roman World*, Units I and II (Cambridge UP, 1978–9, OP)

Clayton, P.A. (ed.) *A Companion to Roman Britain* (Phaidon, 1980, OP)

Cunliffe, B. *Fishbourne Roman Palace* (Tempus Publications, new edn, 1998)
   The Regni (Duckworth, 1973, OP)

de la Bédoyère, G. *Roman Villas and the Countryside* (Batsford/English Heritage, 1993)

Edwards, J. (trans.) *The Roman Cookery of Apicius* (Rider Books, 1996)

Frere, S.S. *Britannia: A History of Roman Britain* (Pimlico Books, new edn, 1991)

Green, M. **Roman Technology and Crafts* (Longman, 1979, OP)

Henig, M. **The Art of Roman Britain* (Routledge, new edn, 1998)
   Religion in Roman Britain (Routledge, 1995)

Ireland, S. *Roman Britain – A Sourcebook* (Routledge, new edn, 1996)

Johnston, D. (ed.) *Discovering Roman Britain* (Shire Publications, new edn, 1997)

Roman Villas (Shire Publications, 1979)

Jones, E.H., Jones, B. and Hayhoe, M. (eds) *Roman Britain*, Themes' Series (Routledge, 1972, OP). An anthology of sources in translation, poetry and extracts from historical novels.

LACTOR Committee *Some Inscriptions of Roman Britain*, LACTOR 4 (LACTOR Committee, new edn, 1995, address below)

Literary Sources for Roman Britain, LACTOR 11 (LACTOR Committee, 1997)

Ordnance Survey *Map of Roman Britain* (new edn, 1997)

Potter, T.W. and Johns, C. *Roman Britain* (British Museum Publications, 1992)

Richmond, I. *Roman Britain*, revd Todd, M. (Penguin, 1995)

Roberts, N. *Roman Britain* Parts I and II. Two folders of source materials (Nicolas Roberts Publications, address below)

Rule, M. *Floor Mosaics in Roman Britain* (Macmillan, 1974, OP)

Salway, P. *Roman Britain*, Oxford History of England Vol. IA (Oxford UP, new edn, 1997)

Sealey, P.R. *The Boudican Revolt against Rome* (Shire Publications, 1997)

Sorrell, A. *Roman Towns in Britain* (Batsford, 1976, OP)

Tomlin, R.S.O. *Reading a 1st century Roman Gold Signet Ring from Fishbourne* (Sussex Archaeological Collections 135, 1997). An important article which suggests a change of name for Cogidubnus.

Wacher, J. *The Towns of Roman Britain* (Routledge, 1997)

Webster, G. *Boudica: The British Revolt against Rome AD 60* (Routledge, new edn, 1993)

The Roman Invasion of Britain (Routledge, new edn, 1993)

Wilson, R.J.A. *Guide to the Roman Remains in Britain* (Constable, new edn, 1988)

Fishbourne Roman Palace

Rudkin, D. *Young Persons' Guide to the Palace* (new edn, 1998)

Ryley, C. *Roman Gardens and their Plants* (Sussex Archaeological Society, 1998)

Exploring the Palace; *Exploring the Mosaics*: Two in-house teachers' booklets for Key Stage 3. All the above publications are available from the site.

Historical novels

Davis, L. *The Silver Pigs* (Pan, 1989). The first adventure of the Roman detective Falco.

Duggan, A. *The Little Emperors* (Faber, 1951, OP)

Kipling, R. *Puck of Pook's Hill* (Macmillan, 1989)

Marris, R. *The Cornerstone, Long Ago Series (Heinemann, 1979, OP). A story about the son of a Fishbourne mosaicist.

Plowman, S. *To Spare the Conquered (Methuen, 1960, OP). Set at the time of the conquest of Britain and Boudica's revolt.

Ray, M. *The Eastern Beacon (Faber, 1965, OP). The adventures of a young Greek girl and Roman boy who are shipwrecked on the Scilly Isles in the 3rd century.
*Spring Tide (Faber, 1979, OP). Two boys encounter Christianity for the first time.

Seton, A. *The Mistletoe and the Sword (Brockhampton, 1956, OP). Set at the time of Boudica's revolt.

Sutcliff, R. *The Eagle of the Ninth (Oxford UP, new edn, 1998). A young Roman officer tries to recover the lost eagle of the vanished Ninth Legion.
*The Silver Branch (Oxford UP, new edn, 1998). Sequel to the above, set 170 years later.
*The Lantern Bearers (Oxford UP, new edn, 1998). A Roman soldier remains after the withdrawal from Britain and helps to fight the invading Saxons.
*Outcast (Oxford UP, 1998). A young British tribesman is sold into slavery.

Treece, H. *Legions of the Eagle (Puffin, 1970). The story of a boy living during the invasion of AD 43.
*War Dog (Brockhampton, 1962, OP). A story about Bran, the huge war dog of Caractacus' charioteer.
*The Queen's Brooch (Hamilton, 1966, OP). The life of a young Roman who encounters Boudica.

Wheeler, M. *The Farthermost Fort (Dent, 1969, OP). This story centres on the final withdrawal from Britain.

Alexandria and trade

Badian, E. *Ancient Alexandria (History Today 10, November 1960)

Clayton, P. and Price, M. The Seven Wonders of the Ancient World (Routledge, new edn, 1990)

Ellis, S.P. *Graeco-Roman Egypt (Shire Publications, 1992)

Evans, I.O. *Gadget City (Warner, 1944, OP). A novel about a Welsh slave captured in Britain and sent to work at the Museum in Alexandria.

Forster, E.M. *Alexandria – A History and Guide (M. Haag, new edn, 1981)

Fraser, P.M. Cities of Alexander the Great (Oxford UP, 1996)

Lindsay, J. Daily Life in Roman Egypt (Muller, 1963, OP)

McLeish, K. *The Seven Wonders of the World (Cambridge UP, 1989)

Meiggs, R. Roman Ostia (Oxford UP, new edn, 1985)

Riche, W. La Alexandria: The Sunken City (Weidenfeld and Nicolson, 1996)

Romer, J. and E. Seven Wonders of the World (O'Mara Books, 1996)

Steen, G.L. (ed.) *Alexandria: The Site and History* (New York UP, 1993)

Thorley, J. *The Silk Trade between China and the Roman Empire at its Height, c. AD 90–130* (Greece and Rome 18, April 1971)

Walker, S. and Bierbrier, M. **Ancient Faces: Mummy Portraits from Roman Egypt* (British Museum Publications, 1997)

Religion

Apuleius **The Golden Ass* (trans. Graves, R., Penguin, 1990; trans. Kenney, E.J., Penguin, 1998; trans. Walsh, P.G., Oxford UP, 1995)

Harris, G. *Isis and Osiris* (British Museum Publications, 1996)

Lindsay, J. *Men and Gods on the Roman Nile* (Muller, 1968, OP)
Origins of Astrology (Muller, 1970, OP)

Robertson, O. *Isis Wedding Rite* (Cesara Publications, 1976, address below)
Rite of Rebirth: Initiation of the Fellowship of Isis (Cesara Publications, 1977)
Dea – Rites and Mysteries of the Goddess (Cesara Publications, 1979)
The Call of Isis (Neptune Press, new edn, 1993)

Takacs, S.A. *Isis in the Ancient World* (Johns Hopkins UP, new edn, 1997)

Medicine, science and technology

Bynum, W.F. (ed.) *Dictionary of the History of Science* (Macmillan, new edn, 1997)

Davies, R.W. *Medicine in Ancient Rome* (History Today 21, November 1971)

Dodsworth, R. **Glass and Glassmaking* (Shire Publications, 1982). A short illustrated history.

Hill, D. *A History of Engineering in Classical and Medieval Times* (Routledge, 1996)

Hodges, H. *Technology in the Ancient World* (O'Mara Books, new edn, 1996)

Landels, J. *Engineering in the Ancient World* (Constable, new edn, 1998)

Lee, Sir D. *Science, Philosophy and Technology in the Greco-Roman World* (Greece and Rome, April and October 1993)

Loudon, I. (ed.) *Western Medicine* (Oxford UP, 1997)

Majno, G. *The Healing Hand: Man and Wound in the Ancient World* (Harvard UP, new edn, 1991)

Nicholson, P.T. **Egyptian Faience and Glass* (Shire Publications, 1993)

Nunn, J.F. *Ancient Egyptian Medicine* (British Museum Publications, new edn, 1997)

The Schools History Project **Medicine and Health through Time* (John Murray, 1996)

Audio-visual resources

Videos

The Roman Invasion of Britain. 55 minutes. (Focal Point Audio Visual, address below)

Talkin' Roman History Trail. 25 minutes, chat-show style interviews with a Roman centurion, a Celtic farmer and Queen Boudica. Teachers' notes. Primarily for children aged 7–11. (English Heritage, XT 10838)

Steam as it Was. Broadbent, J.E.A./University of Manchester Faculty of Science. The development of steam-powered machines, from Hero of Alexandria onwards. (Available from Manchester University TV, address below)

Posters, photographs and resource sheets

Butser Ancient Farm. Teacher's Pack of photocopiable sheets on many aspects of Iron Age life. Items such as woad seed, heads of emmer, etc. also available.

English Heritage. (No longer publish slides.) The Education Resources Catalogue (2000) (address below) includes:

Roman Britain Poster Pack: 8 posters, 4 in colour and 4 (photocopiable) in black and white. (XR 14040)

Roman Artefacts Picture Pack: 30 colour postcard-size photographs with information on the back and activity ideas. (XR 14041)

Using Roman Sites. Book including photocopiable resource sheets. (XP 10659)

CDs

English Heritage. *Real Romans – Digital Time Traveller.* Interactive CD-ROM and book, exploring a fort (Housesteads), a villa (Lullingstone) and a town (Wroxeter). With posters, Roman board game and activity ideas. (XT 14064)

Slides and filmstrips

Roman Britain

Roman Britain. Cambridge Classical Filmstrip 2, 35 frames, designed to accompany the integrated edition of the *Cambridge Latin Course*, Unit IIA and IIB (Cambridge UP, 1984)

Roman Britain. 50 slides with notes. A general survey of the whole Roman period in Britain (Focal Point Audio Visual Ltd, address below)

Fishbourne Roman Palace. A series of slides is available from the site (address below). A website *Romans in Sussex*, including substantial material on Fishbourne, is planned for early 2001.

Peckett, C.W.E. *Roman Britain.* 43 slides with notes; optional audio cassette. A general survey of the whole Roman period in Britain. (Visual Publications, M11/3, address below)

Todd, K. *Greek and Roman Farming.* 44 slides with notes; optional audio cassette. (Visual Publications, M12, address below)

White, H.A.B. *Camulodunum, Colonia Claudia Victricensis* (Colchester). 40 slides with notes, or as filmstrip. (D.M. White, address below)

Mosaics in Roman Britain. 35 slides with notes, or as filmstrip. (D.M. White, address below)

Londinium. 40 slides with notes, or as filmstrip. (D.M. White, address below)

White, H.A.B. and H.R.B. *Fishbourne Roman Palace*. 36 slides with notes, or as filmstrip. (D.M. White, address below)

Members of the Hellenic and Roman Societies (address below) can draw on their joint library's extensive slide collection and buy the following filmstrips, or hire them as slides:

T.W. Potter. *Roman Britain I: Historical and Military Aspects*. 32 frames with notes.

Roman Britain II: Civilian Life. 35 frames with notes.

Roman Egypt

Bolton, P.H. *Ancient Egypt*: (1) *The Gift of the Nile*, (2) *Empire and Decay*. 44 + 41 slides with notes; optional audio cassettes. May be useful as background, though ending with Cleopatra. (Visual Publications, M4/1,2, address below)

Dalladay, R.L. *The Palestrina Nile Mosaic*. 12 slides with notes. This mosaic shows the Nile in flood, with temples, farmers, wildlife, hunters, shipping, etc. (Ministrips, address below)

Glassmaking and Roman Glass. 16 slides with notes. (Ministrips, address below)

Addresses

Butser Ancient Farm, Nexus House, Gravel Hill, Horndean, Waterlooville PO8 0QE. Website: www.skcldv.demon.co.uk/iafintro.htm

Cesara Publications, Huntington Castle, Clonegal, Enniscorthy, Eire.

English Heritage Postal Sales, PO Box 229, Northampton NN6 9RY.

Fishbourne Roman Palace, Salthill Road, Fishbourne, Chichester PO19 3QR.

Focal Point Audio Visual Ltd, 251 Copnor Road, Portsmouth PO3 5EE.

Joint Library of the Hellenic and Roman Societies, Senate House, Malet Street, London WC1E 7HU.

LACTORS (Ken Hughes), 17 Belgravia Mews, Palace Road, Kingston-upon-Thames, Surrey KT1 2LP.

Manchester University TV, Oxford Road, Manchester M13 9PL.

Ministrips (R.L. Dalladay), Abbey Cottage, East Cliff, Whitby YO22 4JT.

Nicolas Roberts Publications, Long House, Church Road, Wisbech St Mary, Cambs PE13 4RN.

Visual Publications, The Green, Northleach, Cheltenham GL54 3EX.

D.M. White, Priory Farm, Balscote, Banbury OX15 6JL.